TOWER OF THIEVES

AIG

TOWER OF THIEVES

AIG

ANDREW SPENCER

Brick Tower Press
New York

Brick Tower Press
1230 Park Avenue
New York, NY 10128
Tel: 212-427-7139 • Fax: 212-860-8852
bricktower@aol.com • www.BrickTowerPress.com

The Brick Tower Press colophon is a registered trademark
of J. T. Colby & Company, Inc.

Library of Congress Cataloging-in-Publication Data

By Andrew Spencer.
TOWER OF THIEVES, AIG
ISBN-13: 978-1-883283-69-8
LCC# 2009940476

First Edition, December 2009

.

Cover design and typesetting by The Great American Art Company

10 9 8 7 6 5 4 3 2 1

CO

for Lauren and Jill,
two of the strongest women I've ever
had the pleasure of meeting

ACKNOWLEDGEMENTS

It takes a village to raise a child, and I think it's safe to say that it takes somewhere around the same number of people to write a book of this nature. Tops on my list this time around are John Colby of Brick Tower Press and Alan Morell of the Creative Management Group Agency for making this idea a reality.

To my personal Dream Team of free lawyers, I say thank you from the bottom of my money-saving soul: Arnold Spencer, brother and fountain of free legal advice who happens to be an assistant US attorney; Tom Durkin, who doubles as a St. Bernard rescuing wayward travelers when he's not serving as a federal judge; Mark Junell, pledge brother-turned-attorney; Jamie Ranney, who let me use lunch as a retainer; and Aydin Caginalp, who is becoming something of a regular at vetting my books.

The original meeting never would have happened without Richard Ross. My father – George Spencer, CPA – offered a year's worth of accounting courses via email and phone calls in the space of about two months. Bill Bamber, my co-author on *Bear Trap*, counted windows with his son Moro and answered more than one of my business-related questions on this one, too. Bill Welsh had more than a couple of questions hurled at him, which he was kind enough to answer without laughing at my ignorance. Chris Magee and the crew of *Zingara* saved my sanity on multiple occasions. Thank you very much to you all.

Jill, I never could have gotten here without you. Thank you for being you. I love you very much.

Finally, to my good friend John Falcetta, I thank you for giving me the chance to tell your story. The trust you put in me is at once staggering and humbling. I hope I didn't let you down. Piece o' cake, buddy.

AUTHOR'S NOTE

Chor Minar, located in New Delhi, Delhi India, is a less-than-imposing structure, standing just 36 feet tall. Built in the 13th century, it is what is known as a minaret, an architectural feature common to Islamic mosques. Minarets are tall spires with bulbous tops that, originally used as watchtowers, are today used to beckon the faithful to their daily prayers. Most minarets feature numerous windows that once allowed torchlight to shine forth from the interior.

Chor Minar has 225 such windows which, in addition to being openings from which beacons of light were able to shine forth, were also somewhat infamous for another purpose. As was the custom with minarets in India at the time, the heads of captured prisoners — captured prisoners who had been decapitated — were displayed as a warning to those who would cross the local authorities. Many of those executed prisoners were criminals who had been convicted of stealing, and their bodiless heads sitting in the windows of the minaret gave the tower its name, which in ancient Persian means "Tower of Thieves."

The American International Building in New York City at 70 Pine Street — known to many as simply the AIG Tower — is a somewhat more commanding structure than Chor Minar. The AIG Tower soars 952 feet into the sky above lower Manhattan, and has somewhere in the neighborhood of 2100 windows. According to most estimates — and most public opinion polls — the AIG Tower has far too few windows to adequately display the heads of the thieves inside. With all due respect and homage to Chief Brody from *Jaws*, we're gonna' need a bigger building.

December 18, 2007, Nantucket, MA: FBI agents and local police arrested John J. Falcetta, a former vice president with AIG's life insurance division. He was scheduled to be arraigned Wednesday in federal court in Boston.

Arrested separately were Gary J. Santone and Thomas Pombonyo, while a fourth defendant, Justin Broadbent, was still being sought Wednesday.

"Beyond stating that we're cooperating fully with the authorities, I would decline to comment," said Michael Arcaro, of AIG's media relations department.

Photo by Jim Powers/*The Inquirer and Mirror*

FOREWORD

On the morning of December 18, 2007, I was twenty-eight years old and eight months pregnant with my third child. My husband had lost his job in New York City, and we were living in Nantucket, Massachusetts. My oldest son, Porter, had gotten up early, as was sort of his custom. Though exhausted from a relatively sleepless night – an unavoidable side-effect brought on by the discomfort of being gigantically pregnant – I got out of bed, poured him some milk and agreed to let him watch a little TV in our bedroom. My husband had fallen asleep downstairs the night prior. On the nights that happened, he would sleep in the guest room to avoid waking anyone up. As I was flipping through the channels, I remember feeling sort of unsettled, anxious even, like the air was really thick. I suppose it could simply have been that I was weeks from giving birth and so just a little off. Or perhaps it's that thing we all have, that sixth sense when something is coming. Or maybe it's just that hindsight is 20/20.

"Stop here! Stop here, Mommy! I want to watch this!" As I lifted my thumb off of the channel button and looked up, I saw a giant, yellow, break-dancing bear in gold chains and a side-cocked hat. He was called Hip Hop Harry, and he appeared to be doing some educational rapping. He kept saying, "I love to learn! I love to learn!" While giant bears – and giant rapping bears at that – are unsettling all on their own, it was not Harry who had contributed to that earlier sense of foreboding that had so overwhelmed me. It was instead what came just moments after.

Out of the corner of my eye, I noticed something at the top of our driveway. As I moved closer to the window, I saw three black SUVs barreling down the drive. I heard the crunch of the crushed white shells beneath their tires as the mammoth cars approached the house. I glanced at the clock. It was 6:45 AM. For a split-second, I thought that maybe this early morning visit was related to the construction ongoing on another part of the property. I glanced back out the window. The vehicles had stopped in front of our house. Five or six men were slamming their doors. I saw them coming up the walkway, their strides indicating a sense of purpose. There was a banging on the front door, followed by, "FBI. Open up!" They were definitely not here to do construction.

I heard my husband's heavy feet across the floor below. "I'm coming!" he shouted.

With my stomach in my throat and unable to think, I picked Porter up from in front of the television and walked to the top of the steps in complete and total disbelief. The door opened and, much like in the movies, there was a man in black with his badge outstretched saying, "FBI." The steps to our second floor led right down to the front door. After the agent at the front of the pack finished saying, "John Falcetta, you're under arrest," he looked up the steps at me and said, "Ma'am, you should leave the children upstairs."

Completely unaware of what was taking place just steps below him, Porter resumed his position in front of the TV. Terrified and confused, I walked downstairs. The agent told John that he was being taken to Boston on a matter out of New York.

John kept asking, "Can you tell me what this is about?"

The agent just kept saying, "It's a matter out of New York." He gave no other details, no matter how many times John asked.

Having just woken up, John asked if he could at least get dressed and use the bathroom. The agent agreed to let him, but told John that he was not permitted to be alone at any time, and would thus have to be attended by an FBI agent. The agent who drew that duty watched him pee and put on his pants. He advised him to wear shoes without laces. John left the house that morning in a button-down shirt, warm-up pants and dress loafers.

Meanwhile, the four or five other agents were all wandering around our living room. I noticed one man pick up a photo of one of my children and look at it. I stood there, silently willing him to put it down. Though they were probably just a group of guys doing their jobs, as they meandered through my home that morning, touching my things, they just seemed like the enemy and I felt violated.

I don't want to say it seemed like overkill for there to be so many of them, but it seemed like overkill! We joke about it now, that maybe they thought there should be ample back-up in case John gave chase. My husband is funny and smart and fantastic, but one thing he certainly is not is a healthy tri-athlete.

In retrospect, it's funny the seemingly insignificant things I recall from that horrible morning. For instance, I remember that the lead agent had a clipboard and papers, but no pen. He picked mine up from the counter and began to fill in his paperwork. He didn't even ask. And then when he was finished, he just rolled the pen off of the clipboard and back on to the counter. I know how ridiculous it seems to have been outraged by the FBI agent's lack of pen etiquette at a time like that, but I think I was in such a state of shock and disbelief at what was happening that I just tried to wrap my thoughts around anything I could until it was all over. Maybe I should've just gone into labor right then and there! That would have shown them! Like I said, I know they were just a group of guys doing their jobs, but in that moment, they were my sworn mortal enemy.

"Do you know where I'm going to go from here?" John asked the agents. "Is there any information I can give my wife?" They allowed him to write down the name of the Assistant US Attorney and the phone number for John's personal attorney. Then they told me that he would be at the Federal Court House in Boston later in the afternoon, and would likely be back home by the end of the day. As it turned out, it would be four very long days until John was back home. This was something that in my wildest dreams – or my worst nightmares – I couldn't have imagined.

I remember the agent saying to John, "You've been very cooperative, so we're not going to cuff you." I was standing by the bottom of the steps as they led him to the door. John reached over and put his hand on my giant belly, looked up at my face and said, "Everything is going to be fine. Nothing to worry about. Totally fine." It was vintage John. No matter the obstacle he's staring down, he believes that everything will turn out great. A fleet of FBI agents standing in our house taking him into custody, and John is reassuring me that everything would be fine.

He walked through the door with the agent holding his arm, and the remaining agents following behind. After the door closed, I walked to the window and watched as my husband stood in the front yard, wrists together, awaiting the cuffs they said they wouldn't use. They couldn't have been in my house for more than fifteen minutes, but it was a big fifteen minutes. A life-changing fifteen minutes.

They pulled out of the driveway and I watched them go. Once they were gone from sight, I was immediately hysterical. It was too early to call the attorney or anyone else, really. I started thinking about breakfast. Pancakes, I decided. Definitely pancakes! With a box of pancake mix in my hand, I sat down on the kitchen floor and sobbed. It was a completely overwhelming sort of sobbing, with intermittent periods of hyperventilation. And then I heard my younger son Winny calling from his crib. Not wanting my boys to see me so wrecked and helpless (if a year-and-a-half and a three-year-old can even comprehend those emotions), I wiped my face and became my own coach.

I kept telling myself, "You can do this. You can do this." I didn't really know what I was doing, but whatever it was, apparently I could do it. Calmly and quietly I brought the boys down to breakfast. We ended up having cereal, as the pancakes were more than I could cope with at that moment. I combed their hair and brushed their teeth and got them dressed. I dropped Porter off at pre-school and took Winny to an early-morning play group.

I had the attorney on redial, and I kept pushing that little rectangular button about every twelve seconds until I got a human being. I think it was 9 AM – more than two hours after it had all happened – before I got him on the phone. I recounted what had happened that morning. He asked me if the agents had said what the arrest was related to. All I knew was that it was "a matter out of New York."

In all of it, I wasn't really that concerned with what John had done. I know that sounds strange. It turns out there is a whole lot about my husband that I didn't know, but the things I did know – the things that I continue to know – is that he is sweet and kind, a devoted husband, a wonderful father and is a truly good person at his core.

As I masqueraded through that day, each step seemed more unreal than the one that came before. I was particularly grateful for my children and their train tracks that needed my help in assembly and their sippy cups that needed refilling. The welcome distractions of their everyday lives kept me from falling into a thousand pieces.

Months earlier, when my husband lost his job with AIG, he told me that they had accused him of misusing his company credit card. He told me that it was much larger than the fact that he hadn't reimbursed the company for the iTunes he had downloaded on his card before a flight to China. He told me there were things going on within the company that were wrong. Really wrong. He didn't elaborate on what those things were, but he mentioned that he had been trying to fix them prior to his dismissal. He believed that that may have had something to do with his being asked to leave the company.

My husband is a hard worker. Obsessive, even. While he was with AIG, he worked long hours and traveled extensively. He took phone calls from his boss on Christmas Eve. He missed birthdays and anniversaries and dinnertimes with the family because he believed in the work he was doing. He has a million ways to build it bigger and better and more efficiently, no matter what "it" is. When I tried to wrap my head around what all of that badge showing and hand cuffing could have been about, I was at a loss. All I could come up with was that maybe it had something to do with the "wrong" he had mentioned in earlier months.

I really believed that we would just move through all of this privately. That John would go to Boston and come home and no one would have to know. By midday, I still had not heard from John. The attorneys were still "working on it." After the afternoon pick-up from pre-school, I took the kids to lunch. They had very large grilled cheeses. Even now I remember thinking a sandwich that size could feed an entire family. I ordered two. In the middle of lunch I got a text message from a friend that read, "Do you need anything?" Living on Nantucket proves challenging if you're budget conscious or you like to buy in bulk. Naturally, when I received that message, I thought that perhaps my friend was over on the Cape at the BJ's Wholesale Club and just wanted to know if she should pick up a box of diapers for me.

I texted back, "No. I'm good."

Moments later, "Are you sure? Let me know if you need anything."

Very much in denial about the possibility that word had already spread and the island knew about our morning, I wrote back, "Super. Thanks."

Less than an hour later, that same friend called and said, "Lauren, it's on the Internet. There's a picture of John with federal agents being put on a plane. My sister-in-law called to tell me. He's being charged with embezzlement and mail fraud."

I asked her not to tell me any more. It couldn't be true. That wasn't my husband! Certainly he was sometimes a bit brash, impulsive, kind of a feather-ruffler, but not a criminal! Two days later that same story showed up on the front page of the newspaper. I never read what was online or bought a copy of the newspaper. Instead, I waited.

I wanted to hear it from John.

The calls kept coming. My girlfriend who I had seen at playgroup and preschool drop-off called late that afternoon to find out if I knew that the kids were putting on their holiday sing that night and whether or not I thought they needed to be dressed up for it. I had Porter's outfit laid out, a blue button-down with a red sweater vest and khaki pants. She concluded the conversation by saying, "Didn't you say John was away on business this morning?"

I answered that yes, I had said that.

Hesitantly she asked, "Do you know where John really is?"

I answered that yes, I did know.

"Did you want to talk about that?"

Needless to say, I did not. By this point, I knew that John was in Boston. But I had no idea about his exact whereabouts. The "later today" that the agents had talked about early that morning had come and gone. At 6 o'clock, I was still waiting for "more information" from the attorney and preparing to take my son to sing Christmas carols with his classmates.

There is nothing more precious than a group of sweet-faced three and four year-olds trying to remember the choreography that is supposed to go with Jingle Bells. It almost made me forget that it was now nighttime and I still had no idea where my husband was. Halfway through the performance, I felt my phone vibrating in my pocket. I picked Winny up and darted outside to answer the call. The news was not what I had been hoping for. Because we had recently sold our home and were renting, there was no property to attach a lien to in order to secure the bail. John was considered a flight risk. He would be at the Plymouth County Correctional Facility until they could determine a bail amount. There was something so heartbreaking about my little boy surrounded by his friends having the most wonderful time while his father was in a jail.

The following day I received another call from the attorney. He said John had met with Pretrial Services. He explained that they were a neutral party and it was their job to make a recommendation for the bail and John's release. He told me that John was charming when he met with the woman and that she might be the saving grace that got him home in time for the holiday. She would be calling me to verify some information about John. He reminded me to be completely truthful.

Jeanna from Pretrial Services called me that afternoon. It was such an unfortunate conversation to be having, but there was something so pleasant about her that I almost didn't mind. She asked me to verify a few things: how long had we been married, where had we lived, how much money was in our checking account, all very benign sorts of questions. She then asked me to confirm that my husband had attended the University of Rochester for two years before being dismissed. To that point, I not only thought my husband had graduated from the University of Rochester, but that he had graduated with honors. I also believed that he had gone on to acquire an advanced degree in economics from another very prestigious school. They don't give high-powered corporate jobs to college drop-outs, so this had to be a mistake.

I paused before answering, not sure of what to say. "My husband and I only met in 1999," I finally managed to stammer. "It is difficult for me to verify anything prior to that time."

She continued. "I also have listed that your husband filed for personal bankruptcy in 1988, was convicted of a felony but given probation, and that his first marriage was to a woman in Baltimore and lasted about two years."

If anyone had been in the room, I would have asked them to pick my jaw up off the floor. All of this was news to me. I echoed my previous answer, in what was almost a reflex action: "It is difficult for me to verify anything prior to 1999."

"Can you verify your husband's Social Security number?" she asked. I recited the number back to her; what she had on file was one digit off. I chalked it up to a clerical error. My brain was already overloaded by the morning's events, and I couldn't conceive of any more fraud at that moment.

While I was having this conversation with the good-natured Jeanna, the details of my husband's crime were still more or less a mystery to me. After I hung up the phone and pondered the notion of my husband the bankrupt and felonious divorcee, I was beginning to think he, too, was a mystery to me. I loved my husband, and while I wasn't sure who he had been from 1988 to 1999 – or maybe even from 1999 to the present – I was sure that I loved my husband. And that he loved me.

That Friday I flew over to Cape Cod from Nantucket and took a cab to Boston for John's bail hearing. I kept praying that all would go according to plan. Christmas was getting close, and I was worried that he might not get home in time, that he might be spending the holidays with a bunch of drug dealers in Plymouth County lockup. I have no doubt that there are lots of lovely drug dealers out there, but if one has the choice, being apart from them – regardless of how nice they may be – is far and away preferable.

John's attorney met me outside of the courtroom. He was a little man in a Gucci belt. He carried with him a very big bag, and he had a head of what looked to me like very strange hair. He launched into the standard repertoire that I'm sure he reserved for spouses of his clients: "Well, here's how it's going to go. Pretrial has recommended that John be released on bail and electronic monitoring. A bail number has been agreed upon, so basically it is just a matter of presenting the information to the judge and then John can go home." Having completed that part of his speech, he turned into a tour guide of sorts. "Have you ever been here before?" he asked me. "It's a nice building."

I finally stopped him. "I'm just a regular sort of girl from a small town in Pennsylvania. I've never been in a courthouse of any kind anywhere. Incidentally, I don't even know what John has done."

"Oh, well, here you go," he replied, handing me a manila folder crammed full of papers. "You can read the complaint. Basically these white collar crimes are how very well-educated corporate types get themselves into trouble."

As I half-read the papers and half-listened to John's attorney's explanation, I paused over that bit about John being referred to as "well-educated." I had learned something very different just the day before. As I continued reading, I came to the part about John's co-conspirators. Up until that point, I hadn't really thought about whether or not there were other people involved. And if I had ever stopped to do so, I certainly never would have imagined that the co-conspirators could have been the people listed. I read over the names again. I knew these people. They had been to our wedding, they had vacationed at our home. I sent them Christmas cards every year with our family photos on them! Shock was starting to feel like my baseline emotion.

As we entered the courtroom, we were informed that there was another hearing that was scheduled just before John's. Three women sat on the left side of the courtroom. The defendant entered, hands cuffed, ankles shackled. After they released his hands, he sat down with his lawyer. The judge entered, everyone rose (much like I'd seen on television). The judge was a fantastic looking woman, very well put-together. I tuned much of that hearing out, but I did happen to catch the mention of a sawed-off shotgun and the selling of crack. There were apparently a number of prior offenses which the defendant and his attorney claimed not to recall. I'm pretty sure that gentleman was not released on bail. Though I was learning all sorts of unexpected things about my husband, I was positive that his hearing would not have anything to do with illegal firearms or drugs.

John's entrance into the courtroom that day was worse for me than his arrest had been. For me, my husband had always been the embodiment of strength and capability. He is a born leader, resilient, seemingly fearless, always in control. He is the sort of person you can knock down a hundred times, but he'll just keep getting back up. As he walked into the room, hands cuffed, wearing green prison scrubs, he looked over at me and mouthed the word, "Hi." He looked tired and ashamed. He looked helpless and lost. All very un-John-like adjectives to be sure.

They moved through the hearing with little fanfare. Both parties were in agreement. Bail was set at $50,000.00, and John was ordered to wear an electronic monitoring device. Just as things were about to wrap up, a man from Pretrial Services addressed the judge. He stood up and requested that the court take into consideration that the defendant's wife – that being me – was due to give birth in the next few weeks, and that allowances be made for him to accompany her to the hospital for the birth. The judge agreed. I believe she also offered me her congratulations and best wishes.

And that was it. For the time being, anyway. John was free to go and we would have Christmas and a baby. Together, as a family.

John's attorney took me downstairs to wait for him. He kept talking about his big country house and how his wife liked to put a Christmas tree in every room, and then put stuffed animals around the bottom of every tree. From the way he talked about the house, he made it sound like there were eight thousand rooms, each with its own corresponding Christmas tree. He told me about how his dog has a really super, fantastic dog run, too. I just remember thinking it was all kind of absurd small talk and not entirely appropriate for the situation. In fact, I found it completely inappropriate for the situation, but I suppose it wasn't a completely alien setting to him the way it was to me.

A year later, when we met again for John's sentencing, he was still talking about those stupid Christmas trees. I found it to be even more inappropriate the second time around. The first time he'd been talking about this grand spread of his, we were on the verge of losing just about everything; the second time he started in on it, we actually had lost everything. We were living in a 1200 square foot condo with royal blue carpeting outside of Reading, Pennsylvania, a far cry from the house we had left in Nantucket. My Mercedes had become a used Ford. My husband was on his way to prison and we were applying for government healthcare assistance, because the last of our money had gone to funding the attorney's wife's Christmas tree obsession. Much more inappropriate the second time.

After the hearing, we rented a car to drive back to the Cape. I drove. John just kept saying, "I'm sorry." I didn't even know where to begin.

"It said you had aliases," I finally said. "I read the complaint. What could you need an alias for?"

"You know, sometimes when you're on the Internet and you're researching something, maybe you fill in a different name to avoid being spammed later on. I did that a few times. They track those things. That's all they meant."

He was lying and I knew it. I had just come all the way to Boston to be his support, and he was now lying directly to me. "If I'm going to stand behind you," I scolded him, "I have to know who and what I'm standing behind. You have to tell me everything. Truthfully." From that point on, that car ride – which we'd taken God only knows how many times before – was the setting for quite a story. It was as if John had opened the floodgates of truth, and it came pouring out.

In the months that followed, the truth-telling became just as addictive for him as the lying had been all the years before. An unstoppable conscience-clearing, a sort of soul purging, began. In those months, I not only learned about my husband's personal dishonesty, but also about the dishonesty of an entire corporate culture. I learned about a corporate machine that is fueled almost entirely by human greed and an absence of ethics. John was repentant for what he'd done; AIG was silent on the matter.

They say hindsight is 20/20. And if I had been looking for my husband to be something other than the man I had married, I am sure that I would have seen all of this coming. John is a smart, accomplished, powerful sort of presence. While he may not have put in the time to earn a degree, he put in the time to make himself an expert. He has an insatiable thirst for knowledge and a tremendous capacity to not only retain information, but to learn it, to digest it, to make it practicable.

And he is believable. Above all else, he is believable. I didn't question how we could afford the back and forth between Nantucket and New York, because he had a fantastic position with an insurance giant. I just thought that he was probably such an asset that they paid him well. Looking back, I do recall the application process for AIG. I remember him being unsettled at having to fill out a formal application. He was worried about a background check. I thought he was just having job search jitters, just second guessing himself.

And I remember a time when he asked me to drop a check off at the bank when I was out on errands. The name on the check was the company of one of the men who I later would see listed as a co-conspirator. I did ask why he had sent him a check. John's response was that he had done some consulting for him. I could have asked what sort of consulting, and I could have asked when he found the time for extra work. But I didn't. I wasn't looking for it. I didn't want to find it.

When he bought a boat and started talking about a vacation house in Italy, I asked how we could afford those things. He said that he got a bonus. Given the amount some of the executives I'd read about in the newspaper had received as bonuses, it all made sense to me. Or at least it made sense to me then.

How do you not know that your husband was married before you? I knew that John had had a long-term relationship prior to our meeting. He had even said once that they were together so long that it was considered a common-law marriage in the state of Maryland. I guess I could have asked more questions. Things like the details of their engagement or if they had ever planned a wedding. But I didn't. That wasn't what I wanted to see.

Maybe hindsight is 20/20. Or maybe it was all staring me right in the face.

What I wanted to see was a smart, accomplished, hard-working, funny husband and father who loved his family beyond measure. Interestingly, now that the truth is out, I see that same man. Except this time, he has the capacity to see the beauty in what's ordinary. He has the capacity to see greed as destructive. He has the capacity to see what is wrong and dishonest in the world, but more importantly, he now has the desire to do something about it, to make things as right as he can. And what's more, he blames no one but himself for his troubles.

His story as it is told here is a tragedy in every sense of the word. A tragedy, in terms of its strictly clinical definition, is the story of a hero who suffers complete destruction as the result of his own tragic flaw. My husband will be the first to admit that he brought on his own demise, and I think his circumstances as a convicted felon speak to the extent of his personal destruction. He went from a six-figure salary to making nine cents an hour teaching convicted felons at a federal prison.

But as I said, John is more than a greedy and dishonest businessman, though that is how many would like to portray him. He is a husband, a father, a son. There is a part of him in all of us. He is an everyman, and that quality is what makes his story a perfect tragedy. Because there is a piece of John in every one of us, we can learn from his downfall.

To keep things in perspective, when I say that we lost "everything," I mean the material everything, the life that we knew. But we still have each other, three beautiful little boys and the opportunity to get it right on the next go-round. And that's the real everything. So maybe we didn't lose anything at all. I've learned through this ordeal that it's a matter of how you look at things as much as anything else. There are days that I want to sit and cry, to sob without regard for anything around me like I did that morning sitting on my kitchen floor in Nantucket. But then I remember how blessed I really am to have all that I do. It is a lesson I have learned the hard way, but one which I do think I have learned well.

As for my husband's experiences, if there is any good that can come out of that ordeal, it is that he can serve as an example of what can happen to anyone with too much ambition that gets tangled up in a web of corporate greed and succumbs to the easy way out. If, on the other hand, we don't learn a lesson from John's experiences, then the tragedy that has already unfolded will be doubled.

Lauren Falcetta
Reading, Pennsylvania

PREFACE

I was first introduced to John Falcetta when I was working on another book, *Bear Trap: The Fall of Bear Stearns and the Panic of 2008*. Word had gotten around that I was writing the book and everyone, it seemed, had an opinion on what caused Bear Stearns to collapse. And everyone, it seemed, wanted to share those opinions with me. I assured them that I was working with a former Senior Managing Director from Bear, a gentleman by the name of Bill Bamber. I assured them that I didn't need any more information – insider or otherwise – on the firm. But offer they did, all with the best of intentions. And truth be told, every once in a while a real gem of information would appear. But for the most part, it was different translations of what Bill and I were already writing.

Our goal with *Bear Trap* was to have the manuscript done in six weeks, quite an arduous task by any account, and all of these well-meaning offers of assistance were more often than not infringements on my time, which was rapidly getting away from me. So when my phone rang one morning, I was hesitant to agree to a meeting with a man that said he had information I might be interested in. I began my scripted speech about how I didn't need any more information about Bear, that I was doing just fine on my own.

"I didn't work for Bear Stearns," he told me.

Okay. So I'm on an insanely tight deadline and some joker wants to tell me about information that I "might be interested in," but it's not about the project I'm working on? This better be good.

I agreed to a cup of coffee – the writer's lifeblood in situations like this one – because, after all, I could use a good jolt of caffeine and a fifteen minute break from the computer. We found each other pretty easily – he recognized me from a photo that had appeared in the local paper about the book – and he asked if we could go "somewhere more private" to talk. Part of me thought this was ridiculous. A big part of me, in fact. All this cloak-and-dagger nonsense seemed out of place in early summer Nantucket, Massachusetts, of all places. But there was some little sliver inside that told me this could be good. So I went along with it.

We went to a park, sat down and, once we'd gotten through the formalities about how the Bear book was going, we got down to business.

"I should tell you that I've got a sentencing date in a couple of months that is going to result in my reporting to federal prison at the beginning of next year," he began in the same tone of voice he might use to discuss last night's Red Sox game or his thoughts about how the fishing had been so far this summer.

In my admittedly limited experience with such introductions, I have to say that any time a conversation starts with someone's announcing their impending sentencing date, fasten your seatbelt, because the story that follows is usually related to something pretty big, and it's also usually a pretty interesting story that's worth missing a deadline or two to hear.

I took notes as John rolled out his story, the same story you're about to read here. After about five minutes, though, I realized I was no longer writing. I was just listening in disbelief to what he was telling me. This meeting took place long before AIG was the poster child for corporate greed and corruption. For that matter, this was before a lot of people had ever even heard of AIG, and even fewer people knew what they did as a corporation. Of course, today the word is out about outlandish executive bonuses and federal bailout money. As of this writing, the United States government owns nearly 80% of AIG, and the company had taken over $170 billion in federal rescue money to fend off its own collapse.

Yes, we all know about these things because they're in the paper and on the news shows every day. But those news reports and those television reporters don't give you the whole story. And it's not their fault. They just don't know the extent of the deception going on behind the limestone walls at 70 Pine Street. In fact, they haven't even scratched the surface yet. And that's a very scary thing to contemplate.

The first line of *Bear Trap* is a direct quote taken from one of Mr. Bamber's last days on the derivatives trading floor where he worked. When it was clear that the firm was spiraling down into nothingness, he said to a co-worker, "You just can't make this shit up." That phrase kept running through my head as I listened to John's tale of corporate malfeasance. Over the course of that first meeting – I quickly forgot about *Bear Trap* deadlines as we sat for over an hour – John regaled me with several war stories of his time within corporate America. And the longer I listened, the more I kept coming back to Bill's comments about the Bear situation. You just can't make this shit up.

One story in particular stuck out in my mind as exceptionally vivid. At one point during his career, John took a position as an executive at a specific firm where, despite his position and his experience in the professional world, he was still looked at as something of a rookie who was subject to corporate America's version of hazing. There is, John explained, a powerful subculture within much of corporate America that dictates that time makes right. And that's time with the firm. Twenty years on Wall Street and six months at a new firm makes six months at the new firm. Nobody cares what you did during the twenty years prior.

There was a woman at this specific firm where John had newly begun who took an immediate dislike to him, a woman who had a pair of decades at the firm to her credit. This woman used her time with the firm to leverage her credibility, fabricating all sorts of gossip about John, which he saw as a way of testing his own patience. No olive branch he could offer her would stop her malicious behavior. So he stewed in his anger, his resentment towards the woman building with every passing day.

And then one day in the executive dining room, John's nemesis was howling about the food that was being served for lunch. A major issue for her was the labeling of the offerings – she had severe allergies to certain foods that she was particularly vocal about – and on this particular afternoon, she was ranting about the sauce on the day's meal as being capable of "killing someone." That triggered the vindictive part of his brain to act.

Some weeks later, John sponsored a group meeting, one where this woman's team would present their expertise on what John referred to as "some horseshit topic that nobody gave a rat's ass about." Because the meeting was an all-day affair, John had been benevolent enough to hire an outside caterer to prepare lunch for those assembled, at the firm's expense, of course. John had specifically crafted the menu with his female adversary's food allergy in mind and went so far as to make sure one dish had sufficient signage indicating that it contained the specific allergen. So grateful was the woman that she made it a point to thank John before she began her presentation for his attention to detail and concern for her well-being.

What John hadn't told her was that approximately 60% of the meal contained, to some degree, the same ingredient. Massive amounts of it, in fact. And that special ingredient had been specially prepared by experts so as to mask its taste.

During the question-and-answer session after lunch, she stood at the podium fielding questions from the audience. Gradually the color in her face drained and her eyes took on a distinctly pained expression. A few moments later, she began to belch loudly. This was followed by the expulsion from her mouth of her entire lunch, as she vomited uncontrollably all over the stage and the lectern. She rushed from the stage, headed for the bathroom, while the janitorial staff did what they could to clean the area. Ten minutes later, she hobbled into the room again, her hair disheveled, her face white as snow. In the ensuing five minutes, she had to twice leave the room at a panicked pace, bound for the ladies room.

After her second of these unscheduled departures, she returned to the room and again fielded a question. The assembled audience members noticed, however, that the rear of her skirt was now tucked up and caught in the top her pantyhose. She was, meanwhile, completely oblivious to this latest fashion *faux pas*. One of her devoted staffers rushed to the stage, attempting to reach out and pull her skirt down. The presenter, who was at this point in no mood for any antics from her staff, immediately ordered the staffer to sit down and shut up. The staffer obliged, but the rest of the room was having difficulty restraining their laughter. The woman thought it was because they were laughing at the staffer, and she smiled herself as she turned her back to the audience, exposing her posterior for all to see. And at that exact moment, she was struck with a case of what can only be described as involuntary diarrhea.

The cat-calls were merciless. "Call a doctor!" was a crowd favorite, as was "Somebody get a mop!" Needless to say, the meeting was officially cancelled at that point. The moral of the story was, as John told me, "Don't ever fuck with me. I'm like the Taliban. I will strap a bomb to your desk and blow you away." He blinked rapidly after this brief tirade and, despite the public setting, began shouting, "Allah! Akhbar!" at the top of his lungs. He added a melodramatic villain's laugh for effect. I'd known him for less than two hours, but already I'd figured out that this was not somebody I wanted to cross, for fear of what he might do to me in retaliation.

The powers-that-be at AIG would have been well served to heed that same warning when they had the chance.

"This was the noblest Roman of them all:
All the conspirators save only he
Did that they did in envy of great Caesar.
He only, in a general honest thought
And common good to all, made one of them."

—Julius Caesar, V, 5. 68-72

CHAPTER ONE
Who Is John Falcetta?

Who is John Falcetta?

That's a question that has plagued a lot of people for quite some time. There is a man named John Falcetta that one can point to and declare that he is the person in question. But there's much more to it than that. The answer is much deeper than the collection of atoms that have joined together to create the man himself. He is simultaneously run-of-the-mill and perfectly unique. He is, in many senses, every one of us; he is an everyman.

The world that we all inhabit – the one we share with the human enigma that is John Falcetta – is full of liars, and each one of them knows on some level that one day they will get caught. Every liar out there – I don't care if they're a kid stealing candy from a dime store or the most skilled of all fraud artists – knows their day will come. It's as sure a thing as the sun rising in the morning. Take Bernie Madoff for example. Here's a guy who stole billions of dollars, and once he got caught and was pleading guilty to the charges, he said to the judge, "I always knew this day would come." And he meant it, too. It's possible he didn't know he'd be spending the next 150 years of his life – or as much of that sum that he managed to remain alive – in prison, but he did know that at some point he'd get caught. He knew the end would come just like John Falcetta knew it would come.

And once that day does arrive, the liar is faced with a choice. He can keep on lying because, after all, he doesn't have much to lose. Or he can just buck up and tell the truth. He can admit what he did, pay his dues for doing it and then move on with his life. That's called the process of redemption. And to start that process, to try to right his world and make up for the wrongs he's done and seek his own sort of redemption, the con artist in question has to start with the simple admission of who he is and that he is nothing more than a liar.

And just so that we're clear from the start, I should tell you that John Falcetta is, on one level, nothing more than a liar.

For starters, he exaggerated a few qualifications on his résumé. Let me rephrase that. He outright lied through his teeth about his educational credentials and some of his work history. But, like any good story, there's a backstory here. For better or for worse, John didn't have a lot of the advantages that some of his peers had had over the years, and the lack of some of those advantages started an avalanche of personal failings that forced him into a corner, a corner he was going to have to fight his way out of if he were going to become the person he wanted to be in his professional life. That's not an excuse; it's just the truth. Today he openly admits that he chose the wrong way out of a bad situation that he created for himself.

Of course, those résumé lies were just the beginning. There were plenty of scams over the years, scams that grew in complexity over time and which, oftentimes, were built on positions he'd acquired as a result of lying on his résumé. It was quite the twisted snowball he'd managed to create by the time he was finished.

That said, John Falcetta is also a devoted and loving husband and one of the most dedicated fathers that I've ever had the pleasure of meeting. His commitment to his wife and children is matched only by his commitment to his work. To John's mind, life wasn't exactly fair to him, and he did what he had to do to level the playing field. That's all he was asking for; he just wanted his shot at success. And once he'd gotten into the game, he excelled. A poor rationalization to be sure, but also a sign of an obviously flawed man.

He surpassed all expectations that any of his employers might have had of him, a truth that suggested he'd garnered enough education in his own way to more than make up for a lack of other credentials.

His workplace accomplishments — all of them verified, all of them awarded as a result of actual witnessed performance — reads like a Type-A how-to manual. He was one of the top producers at Merrill Lynch at the age of 23; he was the top regional executive at Liberty Mutual before he was 30; he was elected a principal at Mercer at age 32; he made Senior Vice President at a Lehman Brothers portfolio company at age 36; by the age of 41, he was reporting directly to the Senior Vice Chairman of AIG. These accolades and advancements didn't get pulled out of thin air. They were earned.

And they all just add more fuel to the fire of complexity of the man that is John Falcetta. A former colleague of his said of him, "I have seen a merciless hatchetman and I have seen a man who actually gave his own coat to a bum in the middle of a snowstorm. He's complex."

He is more than just complex, though. He is simultaneously complex and perfectly straightforward at the same time, as evidenced by his merciless drive to get the job done, no matter what the job in question is. He makes no attempt to hide the fact that he is a workaholic who will not stop until the job is done better than it has to be done, no matter the time commitment required of him or the amount of effort he has to expend. In fact, it is that characteristic of his — the innate drive that made him employee-of-the-century material — that made it so easy for him to get away with his lies for so long. Because John was such a talented employee who mastered skills in half the time it took others to merely learn them, employers didn't even think about questioning his credentials. He clearly had the abilities, which he must have learned somewhere. In other words, the finished product looked like what the recipe said it should, so nobody bothered to look behind the curtain. He was interviewed by some of this country's most senior executives, and they hired them. John

Falcetta didn't sneak in the back door; he was invited in and then asked to stay.

A co-worker told a story that demonstrated John's commitment to the job: "One time, we were all in Hong Kong and the phone rang some time after lunch. It was about two o'clock in Hong Kong, I guess. Anyway, it was Falcetta. He was calling from his office in New York. It would have been about one in the morning there, but he was in his office. We all just sat there and shook our heads, but it was just part of John's regular work day." A twenty hour workday was just a "regular" day. That is dedication bordering on maniacal devotion; John's philosophy was that he could rest when he was dead.

How does one begin to defend someone like John Falcetta, someone who made money by scamming others? One can start with basic numbers. Over one hundred victims of Bernie Madoff's massive Ponzi scheme wrote letters asking the judge to hand down the maximum sentence allowed under law; in contrast, there was not a single letter written in support of him, a fact the judge said was "telling."

I don't want to create the idea that John Falcetta is the second coming of Bernie Madoff. They are apples and oranges, two men cut from entirely different cloths who lived entirely different lives after committing crimes of entirely different magnitudes. But both are con artists and both deserve the punishment that they received. I am not a defense attorney, and I don't intend to mount a spirited defense to save John's name. Friends, Romans, countrymen, lend me your ears. I come to neither bury nor to praise John Falcetta. I simply want to tell his story. And if in that telling it sounds as if I'm praising him, then so be it. He is deserving. Conversely, if I sound as if I am attempting to bury him, an argument could be made for the validity of that, too.

As for AIG, I leave it to you to determine if they are worthy of redemption. Much of this story is that of a bad man, a man who conned his way into a lot of money. But there is a whole lot more to the story than just that, because much of the same story is the story of a benevolent man, a man who wanted to do good in the world. He's a man a lot like many of you out there today, in fact. He wanted his wife and children to never have to want for anything. He wanted to give them every advantage that had been denied him in his youth. He didn't set out to hurt anybody or rob anybody or destroy anybody's life. He just wanted to have as good a life as he thought he was capable of and to provide the best life possible for his family and to cover a few sins from his admittedly checkerboard past.

On the outside, John is a con man and a scam artist. He is a thief. He is a liar. He is a convicted felon. There is no defending him from those titles of his past. On the inside, however, he is a good man seeking to do good works in a world that didn't give him the chance when he tried it honestly. Whereas Bernie Madoff had no supporters writing on his behalf, John had over fifty letters written by friends and colleagues, all of whom attested to his strength of character, his excellent work records, his devotion to family and friends. Many of those letters talked of the lives he saved and the companies he saved. These weren't letters from priests or therapists or bartenders. These were letters from people like you and me.

And that is also telling.

*   *   *

John Falcetta was born in Staten Island, New York, on February 3, 1964. His mother was an Irish immigrant sent to live with family in America when her father – John's grandfather – died of a heart attack at the age of forty-one in post-war Dublin. So she showed up in New York at the ripe old age of fifteen and went to work. She married John's father and then became a stay-at-home housewife and mother. She died several years ago of a heart attack at the age of 61, and John oftentimes says that he will go to his grave believing that his mother was a saint. She bore her burden as the wife of a hard drinking New Yorker with a grace and dignity that John says were enviable, and he claims that not a day goes by that he doesn't miss her terribly and thank whatever god it was that sent her down to be his mother.

Mr. Falcetta – John's father – was also named John, a fact that would come in handy down the road for John, Jr. His father, John, Sr., bounced around from mid-level job to mid-level job in New York City. He worked for an airline in their corporate office on Madison Avenue – that's where he met John's mother, actually, as they were working together. That job cemented in John Jr.'s mind the image of his father as an executive, a man who worked on Madison Avenue. It was an image that would stick with John for many years to come.

He then worked for McGraw-Hill in New York City. There was some flavor of a corporate scandal at McGraw-Hill in the early 1970's, and Mr. Falcetta was let go. He never talked about what actually happened or why he was terminated. It was just one of those things that happened and nobody asked why. From there he went to the corporate offices of Hertz, where another scandal involving the Federal Trade Commission ended his career there. Just before he reached retirement age, he worked as a janitor at a local high school, a far cry from his days on Madison Avenue. John, Jr., swore that he would never let the corporate machine do to him what it had done to his father, namely take him in and use him up, only to spit him out on the sidewalk when they'd finished with him. Hatred is a powerful motivator, especially in the case of the younger John Falcetta.

After the death of John's mother, Mr. Falcetta remarried a woman a few years older than his only son, which hurt John in ways that he never knew were possible.

In 1974, John was ten years old. He spent most of that year in and out of the hospital, where he underwent a host of nightmarish medical procedures. He had blood drawn almost daily, often multiple times a day; the highest number of vials of blood drawn from his arm in a single twenty-four hour period was thirty-seven. He underwent radiation treatments. He endured multiple spinal taps. He had his bones drilled into to have marrow extracted. And none of it was ever explained to him. He was never told why, at the age of ten, he was being subjected to tests that, had he been a prisoner of war, would have been outlawed by the Geneva Convention. But because he was a ten-year-old, they were deemed appropriate, though to this day he doesn't know what the reason for them was. No formal diagnosis was ever made.

He slept for up to twenty hours at a time. He was constantly fatigued and lived in a mental fog that never seemed to lift. For the duration of his ordeal, he was never told what the goal of the tests was, nor was he told how long he'd be subjected to them. He just endured. His mother was there every day, by his side, without fail. His father was working to support the family, and was only able to come by to visit his son evenings and occasional weekends.

And then one magical night – Christmas Eve, 1974 – two men appeared at John's bedside. The two interlopers – John's father and grandfather – wrapped the young boy up in a blanket and, in the most clandestine of operations, secreted him away to the only place he wanted to be, his own home. The next morning, John awoke to a Christmas that he told me John Paul Getty himself couldn't have equaled. Sitting in his parents' living room on Christmas morning was a bicycle – a Schwinn, complete with a banana seat and streamers – not to mention a new football, a Washington Redskins banner (John's favorite team), an electric train set. In short, everything a boy of ten could possibly want. "In the end," John said, "that's how I will remember my father. For that one act of kindness. For what he did for a sick little boy."

As a child, John tested off the charts in both reading and math. At one point, his teachers tried to convince his father to allow him to take college-level courses as a fourth grader; alternatively, they wanted him to attend a school for gifted children. Mr. Falcetta declined on both offers; he figured that public school had been good enough for him, and was sure as hell good enough for his kid. As John was to discover growing up, his father was as emotionally complex as John would be as an adult.

So John spent his junior high years in a public school in Staten Island with his less-gifted peers, many of whom saw fit to stuff him into trash cans. John was the brainy kid, the one that the cool kids resented and made fun of. He never quite fit in, no matter how hard he tried. He was either too smart or too uncoordinated or too whatever else that kids decide is important at a given moment. He spent his childhood on the outside looking in, longing desperately to be a part of the group. Like young Charlie Bucket gazing longingly into the candy store, John couldn't manage to find his way in with the other kids.

John's best friend growing up – a young man named Warren – was like him in almost every way. Warren had an IQ of 163, which was a single point higher than John's. Like John, Warren was also a social outcast who didn't have many friends and who never fit in. They were perfect mirror images of one another. The only problem, at least from the standpoint of most definitions of friendship, was that Warren didn't actually exist. He was John's imaginary – and only – friend.

But he got his revenge on them in more ways than one, a character trait that would begin to cement itself as part of his psyche as he got older. There was the time, for instance, when he held a raffle with the kids at school and those in his neighborhood. He sold tickets – twenty-five cents a pop, which was a king's ransom for boys at the time – and the winner would get a brand new car. Mind you, they were all seven or eight years old at the time, so the logistics of the thing were beyond their collective comprehension or concern. All these kids cared about was winning a new car. And John was able to remove any shadow of a doubt they might have had by showing them the car they were hoping to win; he went so far as to hang a hand-made sign on it announcing that it was, in fact, the car they were vying for. It belonged to John's parents, but what these kids didn't know wouldn't hurt them.

In the end, John cleared more money than most eight-year-olds can conceive of, and he would have pocketed all of it if the kid who had won hadn't had the ridiculous notion to show up at his house – towing his parents with him, no less, so that they could drive the thing home for him –asking for the keys to his new car. John's parents were certainly surprised. John told me about the incident: "The little jerk cost me fourteen bucks and earned me a good beating from my old man." Perhaps the battle had been lost, but even a young boy learns as much from his defeats as he does his victories, and John was learning the art of the scam, even at that young of an age.

His parents thought the Cub Scouts might be a better environment for young John, so they signed him up. He played by the rules for the most part, but John was a scammer through and through. After a few months as a Scout, John began going door-to-door selling candy under the guise of raising money for Pack 150. When his customers saw his boyish grin and his perfectly pressed Cub Scout uniform, they were instantly charmed. It didn't matter that the candy seemed a little expensive; it was going to a good cause and helping this nice young man to learn leadership skills that would one day help him in his professional life.

Little did they know how right they were in regards to the prices he was charging for the candy. The price they were paying was actually a dollar higher than what they would have paid to any other Scout who was actually living up to the Scout law that dictated a Scout was honest. John, in contrast to the honorable intentions of his fellow Scouts, was employing the rules of any good retailer and marking up the cost so as to maximize his profit. His personal profit, that is. One dollar went to Pack 150; one dollar went to John's savings account that his father had helped him open. His father had explained to him the concept of earning interest on your savings by "loaning" your money to the bank. He'd told John it was "free money" that the bank would give him. Free money struck a chord in John's young financial brain, and he was hooked.

After graduating from the Cub Scouts to the Boy Scouts, John became quite adept at another scam, one that relied not only on the good reputation of the Boy Scouts of America, but also on that of the United Nations Children's Fund, known as UNICEF to most of us. John would once again don his uniform to perpetrate this little scam. He would stand outside the local grocery store, wearing his uniform, charming the pants off of anyone that came within fifty feet of where he was standing. With just a few words, he'd coax money – big money – out of shoppers who suddenly felt guilty for all they had, especially in light of the fact that children younger than John were literally starving to death. Rare indeed was the shopper who passed the young man with the UNICEF donation box that didn't stuff a bill or two into the narrow slot. With all of the money John raised, you'd expect him to be one of the top money raisers in the country, and it's entirely possible that he was. UNICEF, of course, only got money from John after he'd taken his cut of the action to pay his own "expenses."

The laundry list of John's petty thievery and small-time con games goes on and on. There was the two-year span he worked as a cashier in a deli, selling food and beer out the back door to his friends at discounted rates. And then there was the time he took a job as the manager of a snack bar in a mall in Mt. Kisco, New York. The whole operation was run by three people – John, his assistant, and a "mystery third employee" who never actually showed for work. But because he was the manager, John handled payroll, so the "mystery employee" could be whatever friend happened to be around at the time. It was his first introduction to a "no-show job," where the employee was paid for staying home in exchange for splitting his salary with John. The snack bar had record sales and operating profits under John's direction, despite the fact that he was skimming money off the top.

When the time came for John to head off to college, his father made his position very clear: "I'm not going to become college poor for you," he said to his only son one night. He told John that he could only pay for one of his two kids to go to college; John was, for lack of a better term, the other kid. John had the grades and the public service credentials to qualify for a scholarship if he put his mind to it. His sister would have to have her education paid for, due to her less-than-stellar test scores and grades. Thus it fell to John to figure out how he was going to pay for college himself, if he wanted to go at all.

John was not deterred, nor was he put off. He remembered that Christmas when he was ten, the moment in time that would forever shape his vision of his father. John figured the old man deserved a break and decided that he'd figure out a way to go to college on his own. In his eyes, he was seventeen and on his own. He'd figure out a way to make it through.

The only route he could find was to join the ROTC at the University of Rochester. The ROTC would pay for almost everything he needed. Almost everything. John lasted three semesters before they kicked him out, citing John as a "disruptive influence, both academically and socially." It seems that John, in an effort to make himself some extra spending money, got the idea to solicit money from the parents of his fellow college students in exchange for care packages. Parents could choose from a wide variety of offerings, and John would hand-deliver the packages to the lucky recipients. He would, of course, require payment in advance, as well as a service charge. Long story short, a lot of parents felt sorry enough for their kids to pay for care packages; John didn't feel sorry enough for them, though, and only sent a few of the promised packages after the checks cleared. Despite the entrepreneurial spirit that pervaded his actions, the authorities at the University of Rochester were neither amused nor impressed, and John was summarily dismissed from school.

Through it all – through the Boy Scout scams, the deli counter thievery, the payments to non-existent employees – John learned valuable lessons. And now, having been expelled from school, he'd learned another lesson and had perfected his technique even more, even though the experience had come at the expense of his being dismissed from school prematurely. But despite that, he managed to get enough business knowledge in that time to start him off in what was going to be a twisted and tangled road that would come to be known as a career.

With no college degree – even back in 1984 – you weren't going too far in the business world, especially when "no college degree" was a situation you found yourself in after you got kicked out of school. He needed to clear logistical hurdles if he wanted to get anywhere in life, and clearing those hurdles would require him to cover some of his past tracks. So John began – in earnest – a life of dishonesty that would gradually grow in both scope and complexity. And it all began with one little lie about where he'd gone to college.

John very quickly made the decision that the lack of a diploma was not going to keep him from making his mark on the world, and getting paid well in the process. He went to the Merrill Lynch headquarters in New York City and applied for a job as a stockbroker. He had enough of a business brain to know that buying and selling stocks wasn't rocket science, and "talking some poor schmuck into buying and selling on your schedule was even easier," as John said. The only catch was that pesky missing college degree. But he went ahead and filled out the application anyway, only he filled in his father's college — Wagner College in New York City — in the space where they asked about education. He was applying for a broker's job, so he thought that a graduate program might be a little much of a reach. Not to mention that he was twenty-three at the time, and so probably a little young to have an MBA. But to John's mind, the beauty of this was that if they did decide to verify the fact that John Falcetta had graduated from Wagner College, the reply would come back that he had. He would have to hope that they wouldn't ask what year he'd graduated. But that was a risk he had no control over, and one which he had to take. It was his only chance, and he took it.

The folks at Merrill hired him and he was off and running.

Making cold calls to unsuspecting people is, to be sure, a difficult way to make a living, regardless of what you're selling. The secret, such as it is, is to drive your numbers up. He'd heard Joe Grano, a veritable icon in the industry, say, "Make three hundred dials a day for one year and you will be rich." The theory behind the philosophy was pretty simple: The more calls you make, the more opportunities you have to make a sale. And the more opportunities, the better your final number at the end of the day. John was blessed with a lack of concern for what anybody — especially some random name on the other end of a phone line — cared about him, so he dialed. And he dialed. And he dialed some more. His goal was to make the magic number of three hundred dials per day. He'd dial through lunch, he'd dial long into the night. It didn't matter to him. He dialed.

And it worked. Six months in, John had over seven million dollars under management for Merrill Lynch, as he'd managed to secure the interest of more than one power player in the investment world. He was one of the company's newest rookie stars, impressing all the higher-ups with his work ethic and his results. He was in the top ten percent of all earners, and he had no family money in his accounts. It was all earned through good old-fashioned cold calling of strangers.

And while he was making calls with one ear pressed to the phone, John was using his other ear to listen to those around him, absorbing the techniques, learning the cons that these snake oil salesmen employed. And he incorporated them into his own repertoire, further perfecting his techniques.

Stock brokering is, at least in the minds of a lot of people, the closest you can come to legalized stealing. In its simplest sense, you talk your clients into buying a stock that tickles your fancy at a given moment, and then charge them for the pleasure of doing business with you. When you decide they've lost enough money on that stock, you suggest they sell it and buy a new one. And oh, by the way, we'll be pocketing a hefty commission on both the sale and the buy, thanks for your business. Both the cynical nature of the game and the thinly-veiled element of a scam appealed to John's darker side. He'd found his true purpose, at least for the time being. So impressed were the big guns at Merrill that they encouraged John to get his insurance license. They thought it might instill a little loyalty in him to stay with the company and would also enable him to make even more money for the firm. He got his license and immediately started looking for a better opportunity. And then in 1987, the stock market crashed, and John sought out an easier way to secure clients.

In 1988, John left Merrill to join Chemical Bank in New York, working in the World Trade Center. This was the big time for a kid from upstate New York who had three semesters of college under his belt. This was New York City, with its heavy hitters and drunk Wall Street secretaries. And what's more, he was getting full salary plus commission. A lot more money than Merrill was paying. And as he quickly discovered, they made his job a lot easier for him because Chemical Bank provided the depositor lists to their brokers. So John could look at a sheet of paper and know exactly how much money a customer had and exactly how that money was invested — all the relevant information he needed to manipulate the client's thinking and turn it in a different direction.

The brokers had all sorts of quasi-legal sales pitches they'd use, including use of a trading desk in their office that allowed them to buy and sell different securities while controlling the point spread. So in other words, the brokers could sell a Treasury bill and take a two to five percentage-point commission, but the customers themselves could walk into the bank and buy themselves the exact same security at par, or no points at all. In layman's terms, that essentially means that the brokers were using a sort of grey area to fleece their clients for extra money.

But the biggest – and most lucrative – racket that the brokers were running at the time was the selling of Unit Investment Trusts, or UITs. The UITs at Chemical Bank at the time carried an eight percent commission – not a bad little chunk of change when considering the fact that the initial investment minimum was $100,000. That particular UIT at Chemical offered an actual certificate for the purchaser, so a client would plunk down their hundred grand and get a sheet of paper that said they'd "deposited" the money. The catch was that the bank took its eight percent off the top – so that even though the UIT said its face value was $100,000, the reality was that it was only worth $92,000 after the broker's commission was taken out. But because the certificate was delivered to the client and wasn't held in their account, it didn't show on their statement. It was a trust game with the brokers. Some people might refer to it as a con game, too. Whatever you called it, the client never saw the amount on their statement, and ignorance was bliss. And it was all legal, which made it that much more fun.

Bliss, that is, until the day an elderly woman walked into the bank with her certificate and asked that it be deposited in her account. A month later, the same woman came back to the bank, wanting to know what had happened to the other eight grand she was supposed to have in her account. The upshot of the story was that John was hauled in front of an NASD/SEC investigative committee, but he refused to testify. John was a lot of things; a rat wasn't one of them. The SEC fined him $20,000 for his refusal and gave him a lifetime ban from the business. He took a major hit on the chin for Chemical and Merrill, as he was protecting their trade secrets. Chemical thanked him by firing him. No severance package, no gold watch, nothing.

And with that, John found himself unemployed and broke. He had approximately $85,000 in credit card debt. On top of that, he now owed the government $20,000, plus he was facing a civil suit that Merrill Lynch had filed against him. He had no income with which to pay his rent. And just to add insult to injury, his high school sweetheart left him, bound for a bigger and better Wall Street executive to cater to her needs. He had nowhere to go but up. Or so he thought.

*   *   *

After consulting with a lawyer in regards to the Merrill civil suit and the SEC fine, John declared bankruptcy, as there was no other option that he could see. As a result of having no job and no cash, he got caught passing a couple of bad checks, which resulted in his getting arrested. He didn't have to serve any jail time — it was just a low-grade felony that required paying a fine — but he was taken into custody temporarily and fingerprinted and booked into jail. So now he had both a bankruptcy on his credit report and a felony record on his permanent file. This was not going to make life easier when he set out on the job search again. But like any good businessman, he took it as a challenge. And as any good entrepreneur will tell you, no challenge is insurmountable.

In need of a job — but banned from the world of buying and selling stocks — John stumbled on an odd reality about governmental agencies, namely the fact that they don't communicate with one another very well. So even though he'd had his broker's license revoked for the rest of his life, John's insurance license – the one that the big wigs at Merrill Lynch had encouraged him to get all those years ago – was still fully intact and unaffected by the SEC unpleasantness. So in 1990, John darkened the doors of the MassMutual Financial Group's insurance division, seeking a job as an insurance agent, a job he'd heard about through a connection he'd made during his days at Merrill.

Given his recent financial and legal problems, this was going to be a gamble. But he needed a job, so he rolled the dice. On the application, there was the inevitable question about whether or not the applicant had been convicted of a crime. He left it blank – an oversight by a guy in a hurry to fill out his application, no doubt – and also "accidentally" transposed the last two digits of his Social Security number.

A few days later, his phone rang. It was somebody from the Human Resources (HR) office in Springfield wanting to know about his criminal record. John asked why they were asking. They explained that he'd left it blank – obviously by accident – and they make it a policy to check everyone's home and work state for convictions. John took a deep breath, apologized for his oversight and assured them that his record was clean.

The job he was applying for was in Connecticut, the state in which he was residing at the time. Relying on what he'd learned about the lack of communication between governmental agencies, John thought it was likely states didn't trade information about arrest records. And because his felony arrest had taken place in the state of New York, he could only hope that the authorities in Connecticut had no reciprocity with their neighbors to the south and would have no record of his legal troubles. This was it, he told himself. This was the last time he'd swindle his way into a job. It was a lie he was to tell himself repeatedly over the course of his business life. There were only so many times he could get away with this before he got caught, but he needed a job. So he lied.

And he got lucky.

He began his career as a broker at MassMutual with little fanfare, and slogged his way through the daily grind. John was a mediocre insurance salesman, until one day he stumbled across a way to manipulate the system in a way that spoke directly to him. He was pulling a quote off the printer one day, a quote that another agent was sending out. The quote was showing huge returns, and John approached the agent about it. He wanted to get it for himself, and was curious about what product was offering these exorbitant returns. The answer resonated in his head for the next two years.

"Every product does, young man."

What he came to find out was that when doing an insurance quote, it was the agent himself who determined the return, because the agent projected what he thought the product would return. The computer system the agents used allowed them to put whatever number they chose into the client's projections. So some agents – the more conservative ones in the office – quoted returns in the six- to eight-percent return range, roughly the returns being offered by the stock market over time. The more aggressive salesmen on the force would project ten-percent returns. But this agent would scour investment opportunities, looking for any single product that had offered massive returns over the previous month – the quote in question that John was seeking for himself projected returns of thirty-seven percent – and then selling it to the customer as a product that would consistently return those levels. "Of course it was total bullshit," John explained, "but it was on paper, and clients would believe anything they saw on paper. Their own greed – the clients' desire to make so much money – was what sold it."

John quickly caught on to the technique – which has since been made illegal by updated rules changes – and banged out a small fortune by selling insurance products that no competitor could realistically beat. Of course, MassMutual couldn't realistically make the returns he was selling, either, and the scheme collapsed under its own weight. John found himself on the receiving end of a terse request that he hand-deliver his notice of resignation immediately. But again he was non-repentant. It had been somebody else's fault, he rationalized. Life hadn't been fair to him and he kept getting the short end of the financial stick.

*   *   *

John left Connecticut soon after that and returned to Manhattan, where he did whatever work he could find to keep himself busy. He'd been smarter with his money this time around, so he still had a bit of a savings garnered from the sale of his over-the-top insurance products. Sitting in a bar one night nursing a Stoli on the rocks, John struck up a conversation with the guy next to him. One thing about bars in general, and especially those in New York City, is that they're wonderfully anonymous places. It's almost like going to confession in a Catholic church. You can spill your guts to whomever is there and not worry about it.

And that's exactly what John did. The poor bastard next to him got an earful of his life story. John talked and talked, barely stopping for air. He let it all out, the whole she-bang. The getting kicked out of school. The lying on the job application at Merrill. The multiple firings. The trouble with the SEC. The bankruptcy. And amazingly enough, the guy sitting next to him didn't act in any way judgmental or condescending or negative at all. He just listened like a good barfly. And then he did something very odd.

He smiled.

Not in a mean sort of way that said, "Sucks to be you, you dumbshit," and not in a sympathetic way that said, "Oh, you poor thing, you must need a shoulder to cry on." The only way to really describe it is to say that it was some kind of mischievous – almost evil – grin. So they both sat there for a second in silence, John waiting for the other guy to say something and the other guy just sitting there with that grin. And then he launched into his own life story. A life story that sounded a whole lot like John's own story. Only his sounded even worse than John's. Divorces. Child Support. Scams. Mafia dealings. Multiple bankruptcies. Abortions. Horrible credit problems. Debt collectors hounding him for years.

As this stranger let loose with his own tale of woe, John looked at him for the first time. He noticed that the guy was wearing what looked like a pretty expensive custom-made suit. Definitely not an off-the-rack job. French cuffed shirt with gold cufflinks. An Hermes necktie. A Patek Philippe wristwatch. A pocket square, for Chrissake. Then the thought occurred to him that if this guy had had the problems he claimed to have had in his past, John had nothing to worry about. It wasn't the end of the world that he had initially feared it would be. Obviously there was a light at the end of the tunnel, and this guy was going to be John's guide to getting to it.

At about that point, John felt like they'd developed a pretty good alcohol-fueled friendship, so he asked him about how hard it was to climb out of the hole he'd dug for himself. John wasn't being nosy; he just wanted to have an idea about what his future might look like and when he could look forward to having this guy's kind of money. And most importantly, he wanted to know what it was going to take to get him there.

The guy laughed again. Gave him that same shit-eating grin. "Easy as making a couple of phone calls," he said. And he added a wink as he sipped his cocktail, just for effect. He started to talk about changing who he was, changing his name, changing his whole identity. Changing his life. And this was in

1990, a few years before the Internet was a ubiquitous technology we all took for granted. In other words, this was before every Tom, Dick and Harry knew about identify theft. And that's exactly what this guy was suggesting John had to do. He had to become somebody new – he had to engage in what he called "identity metamorphosis" – if he wanted out of his situation. And John desperately wanted out of his situation. So badly did he want out, in fact, that he was willing to go to any length to get out.

At that moment, John made a conscious decision to leave his old self behind and become someone new, someone who'd never gotten kicked out of school, never declared bankruptcy, never been arrested. Someone who wasn't John Falcetta. And in escaping from his past, he would rebuild John Falcetta in the image that he thought would best suit him and the life he wanted to live.

He rationalized it, as was his habit, by telling himself that it would only be for a little while, just until he got himself sorted out and his personal problems solved. Then he'd go back to being the real John Falcetta. He had no one in his life that would miss him, so what did it matter if John Falcetta became Joe Smith? As Shakespeare said, what's in a name?

That was the moment that, in John's own mind, he started his career as a real charlatan. Yeah, he'd been a con man. Yeah, he'd stolen. Yeah, he'd fudged a little information on job applications. But that was all pretty much a bunch of white lies when compared to what he was about to be doing. What this guy was talking about was full-fledged fraud on a monumental scale; this was going to the edge of reason and taking a flying leap off. He was talking about serious stuff. This was going to be one of those no-going-back moments, when you open the door and step through, knowing that what's on the other side is going to change you forever and there's nothing you can do to get back to your old self no matter how hard you try. This was his own version of the Witness Protection Program.

The alternative – being John Falcetta, convicted bad check writer – involved his owning up to a worthless credit rating and an equally damaging arrest record, not to mention his academic and professional shortcomings. He weighed the options and, when he sat and thought about it, there was no real choice to be made. He had to do what he had to do if he wanted to live the life he wanted to live. And he wanted that life. Desperately wanted it. So he listened intently to what this guy was telling him. And the next day, he walked through that door.

And when a man in John's state – depressed, irrational, delusional – decides to take that first step down that path, the first step is through an enter-only door.

*   *   *

American universities are very trusting places, especially when it comes to making sure that their graduates get jobs. Oftentimes the office in charge of getting students hired at jobs after graduation will believe anything you tell them, so long as it pertains to a student's getting gainful employment that will hopefully result in money being sent back to the university from a gratefully employed new alum. And as a way of illustrating how trusting they are, consider the following story: John Falcetta called the career services office at a prestigious Ivy League university. He told them that he was a New York-based wealth management advisor looking for a new entry-level employee. And much to his pleasure, they couldn't have been more helpful. Was there a particular GPA cut-off he wanted to include? Any specific majors? Was he interested in interviewing undergraduates, or was he solely interested in grad students? Did he want transcripts or just résumés?

They were so helpful, in fact, that they caught him a little off-guard.

He wasn't anticipating all of these questions, so he had to think quickly. He asked for business-related majors, leaving it intentionally ambiguous and letting the woman on the other end of the phone figure out what he meant. He was important, after all, and didn't have the time to be bothered with nit-picky questions that this woman should have the common sense to know the answers to in the first place. He told her he wasn't interested in anybody with less than a 3.0 GPA, and he was open to both undergraduates and graduate students. He didn't mention that he was only interested in male applicants; that request, he thought, might just blow his cover from the start.

About three weeks later, John received a large box in the mail. Inside was a navy blue bound book full of résumés representing the dreams of hopeful soon-to-be Ivy League graduates, all of them anxious to work for him. He started sorting through the contents, looking for a kid who's first name started with the letter J. He didn't care what his last name was, but he was adamant that the kid's first name start with J. If he was going to become somebody else, he figured it would be an easier adjustment if he at least had a first name that began with the same letter. After all, if somebody starts calling you Frank when you've been John for twenty-seven years, you might not respond. But if they call you something that at least starts with the letter J, it's almost just like it's always been.

As it happened, he found a kid who fit the bill. His name started with a J and, as luck would have it, his last name started with an F, too. So he was able to retain something of his original persona. John's new persona had graduated from a well-respected Ivy League undergraduate program with a BA in math, and he was going to be graduating from yet another respected Ivy League graduate program in May with a Masters in Business Administration. He'd spent two years between his undergraduate and graduate years as an analyst at a major New York investment bank. Perfect. John Falcetta had crossed the threshold towards becoming an entirely new person, and he had yet to even break a sweat. He briefly thought to himself that this was coming too easily to him.

Now that he had a name, he needed a background beyond the professional credentials. John quickly discovered that the only people who might be labeled more trusting than university employment counselors are local credit bureaus. After ten minutes of posing as a new lending company, he had a business account at the credit bureau. *And oh, while I've got you on the phone, can I run a quick check on my first client who didn't give me his Social Security number, but I've got his current address.* He read the information directly from the kid's own résumé, and the credit bureau people were happy to oblige their new client. A few minutes later, the picture of John's new life was coming into focus. He now had his new Social Security number, his new date of birth, his new home address. Everything he needed to complete the change in a plan that had been laid out for him by what amounted to a well-dressed drunk at a New York City bar.

As his old life was slowly beginning to merge with his new life, he needed some kind of photo identification. He went to the Department of Motor Vehicles and explained that he'd lost his wallet when he moved to New York, but he needed to get a New York driver's license. No problem, they told him, but he'd need to get a copy of his driving record from the state of his previous residence. He had all the residence information from the credit report, so he made another quick phone call and within a couple of days he had his new driving record. Back to the DMV and within a half an hour, he had a completely new identity. He went to the bank and, with his new ID in hand, opened a checking account and a savings account. And with that, the transformation was complete.

John Falcetta was now somebody entirely different.

John later said that he couldn't believe how easy the whole process had been. It amazed him that people hadn't been more suspicious, and perhaps they would have been in today's world where these sorts of stories seem to come up with an alarming regularity. But again, back then nobody had heard of the Internet, and the idea of being able to rip off someone else's identity was the stuff of spy novels. "Today, people commit identity theft for money," he explained to me. "I didn't want the guy's money. I wanted his name, his life. I wanted a second chance." He laughed for a moment before adding, "Actually it was more like a fifth chance at that point."

Now that he was no longer John Falcetta, a bankrupt bad check writer, he could freely apply for jobs. And with a pair of Ivy League schools on his résumé, John's applications were at the front of every line that he chose to get in. He was getting whisked around the country in private corporate jets, staying at the best hotels, being taken to dinner at the nicest restaurants, playing golf at clubs that he was being assured he could join if he accepted the offer. One firm, in the interest of showing him how much they really wanted him, almost blew his cover entirely. They'd assigned him two "handlers," each of whom had gone to the two schools he was claiming to have attended.

With the best of intentions, these guys were making small talk about specific professors and classes and dorms and whatever else they could think of to talk about from their school days. John, of course, had absolutely no idea what they were talking about, but he faked it well enough and they didn't catch on. Or if they did catch on, they didn't say anything about it.

He ended up taking a job with Paine Webber, serving as an internal consultant advising on issues of that firm's retirement business for brokers. This new job was a perfect fit for John, because it was working with brokers, the only job he'd ever actually been trained for in his entire professional life when he was with Merrill Lynch. The only catch was that he'd never officially been a consultant. But having seen some of the hacks that passed themselves off as professionals in the field, he figured it couldn't be all that hard. So he worked on learning all he could about being a consultant.

He developed his consulting skills and retirement plan knowledge by reading business books in various stores around Manhattan in marathon reading sessions that lasted hours on end. It was, in essence, a crash-course version of a graduate program in consulting. He supplemented his reading with calls to industry experts, who offered him materials that furthered his education. He took everything he learned and paired it with his background with both investments and insurance, and he was immediately accepted as an expert in the field. Things were, he thought, going well. He learned the specifics of the job quickly and he was making good money. But just like everything else on Wall Street, this was easy come and easy go.

He got the call one morning in early March. He was asked to come to his boss's office. He'd been with Paine Webber for about a year and he was doing well, so the last thing in his mind was that he was going to be let go. He'd achieved what he thought was a pretty major part of the corporate American dream: he had a nice office, he was making a great salary, he had a gorgeous Albanian secretary with a penchant for wearing short skirts. Everything was going beautifully for him, at least to his way of thinking.

He walked into the office and immediately knew he'd been caught. There were eight people, all of them standing around his boss's desk, with varying visages of anger and disbelief showing on their faces. His boss cut to the chase right from the start.

"What's your real name?" he asked.

John played stupid at first, asking him what he was talking about. He added what he hoped sounded like a confused laugh to help him pull off the act. This was the moment he'd been dreading since starting this whole journey, and this was going to take the acting job of his life to get out of.

"We know you're not who you say you are," he said. It was painfully clear that he was not calling John by the name that they knew him as. Not a good sign. His stomach dropped through the floor and his heart started beating like mad. "I just got a call from an investigator at the SEC," he went on. "The guy you're claiming to be has a couple of investment accounts here. They cross-reference all of this information, and they were investigating how you managed to avoid disclosing these accounts on your application." The rest of the conversation went by in a blur for John, who felt like he'd been blindsided by a Mack truck. His boss waved his hand toward somebody behind him, and John felt a hand on his arm. "You can leave your company ID here, please. The security officer will escort you from the building."

And just like that, it was over. John Falcetta's alternative life had come to a crashing halt.

He looked straight at the floor as he walked out of the building. He didn't want anybody to know what was going on, though he knew that word would get around soon enough. He didn't feel so much ashamed for what he'd done as he was embarrassed that he'd gotten caught so easily. What are the chances of having the guy whose name you ripped off have a brokerage account at the same firm in a city of eight million people? And what's more, what are the chances that somebody is going to find out about it? Talk about finding a needle in a haystack.

Despite feeling fortunate that the only fallout from the whole event was the loss of his job, he was angry at himself for getting caught. The firm didn't press any charges against him, nor did the SEC follow up with any sort of investigation or punishment. It's entirely possible that his bosses at Paine Weber were just as embarrassed at having been caught hiring a fraud as John had been about getting caught. Either way, the two parted ways and John felt like he'd gotten out of it pretty easily. Even the woman he was dating at the time forgave him, though they, too, later went their separate ways.

So John was once again stuck with being John Falcetta. But he didn't sit around licking his wounds and wondering what might have been. He simply picked up and moved on, and within a few months, he'd hatched a new plan that would help him avoid the issues associated with his old life. He left New York and moved to Baltimore, Maryland, where he applied for a tax identification number, which is a nine-digit number that is just like a Social Security number. With his new tax ID, he opened a checking account and a secured credit card with a $500 deposit. *Voila*, a new credit file was born for John Falcetta. No sweat. He opened a Montgomery Ward account and a JC Penny account, just to give a little bulk to his newly created file. Now he had at least a clean credit history to provide any would-be employers.

He went off on the hunt for a job again, armed with his new credit file and his father's college background. He was playing it safe, for now. He landed a succession of jobs at small firms, and then learned through the Internet — which, by this point, had become the major source of information that it is today — that a major consulting firm was hiring, a firm called Mercer Consulting. The only catch was that the job description said a Master's degree was required. Given the disastrous results with his last try at faking his way through an MBA, he stayed away from that path.

Instead, he opted for something he'd seen on the Internet, namely a Master's diploma you could buy from an operation calling itself The London School of Business, which was, at the time, nothing more than a post office box somewhere in London. With nothing to lose at that point, John plopped down his hundred dollars and bought himself an MBA. It was his own Social Security number, at least. He rationalized in his own mind that it was the start of his turning over an honest leaf in this whole process.

Getting a job with Mercer is not an easy task in and of itself. It requires extensive interviewing and a whole lot of luck, especially if you're trying to scam your way into that job. In John's case, the process lasted from July until October of 1997, and required that he meet with twenty-three different people, pass both a psychological and intelligence test and get through a one-on-one interview with a psychiatrist. He wanted this job badly. Mercer was the best, the absolute top-of-the-line that employed the best and the brightest. He wanted more for himself, a bigger challenge in the business world. He was ready to do anything it took to get the job.

As he progressed through the steps, the stakes grew increasingly higher. John grew more and more concerned that these people were going to catch up to him and the game would be over before it had even really begun, so he worked to out-think the process. The tests that measured his business acumen were easy enough for him. After all, this was the same kid who'd tested off the charts in fourth grade. Those brains had stuck with him through the years. If anything, they'd gotten sharper with age. But the other steps required a great deal of active thinking beforehand if he wanted to get past them.

One day in August of that year, John got a call from a woman in the Human Resources department who was requesting an up-to-date résumé. He agreed to send it in and, in the sort of tone reserved for co-conspirators, he asked her about the process, just so he could prepare. The businessman turning on the old Boy Scout charm. And she fell for it, the poor girl. She told him about the process, and mentioned that there would be a background check. He tried his best, but she didn't reveal any specifics about it. She wasn't going to give it up that easily.

Forewarned was forearmed and, even if he didn't have all the details, at least he had an idea of what to expect. He'd come this far, so he figured he'd see it through to the end. He employed a girlfriend to call the same woman in Human Resources two weeks later to say that she was conducting a survey on employment practices, and if she were willing to participate, they'd reward her with a $250 survey participation fee. All she would have to do was answer a series of questions. And she fell for that one, too. John had a knack for finding co-conspirators as charming as he was.

The woman gave up the information she'd withheld earlier, specifically telling John's accomplice who did the background checks for Mercer and what level of detail they delved into and what specific information they checked. A man of his word, John honored his commitment and sent a money order for $250 to the poor girl. He felt she'd earned it.

Armed then with the information about the company doing the background checks, John found their contact information and called them, posing as the head of a company who was potentially seeking to utilize their background checking services. The sales rep was more than happy to give him chapter and verse on the details of the system, the same information that John would need in order to beat the system. Of course, he was telling him about all the ways the company verified background information, but John's fraud instinct was hearing the subtext, the detailed information about how to get around the checks. Now confident that he could pull it off, John sent in his new-and-improved résumé, complete with the subtle changes that he'd made specifically for Mercer.

During one of his multiple interviews, John picked up yet another tidbit that would prove vitally useful. The head of Human Resources let it slip that John's foreign Master's – the one he'd paid a hundred dollars for – wouldn't hold up his application due to the fact that they didn't verify overseas degrees. "It just costs so much and the goddamn paperwork is unbelievable," he confided. It was just an off-handed comment, something you might say without thinking about it. Clearly the interviewer had no clue who it was he was feeding this information to. John silently filed the information away in his brain, which was already churning and humming as it worked to find ways to exploit this little gem of knowledge.

He was offered the job, and he accepted it without any worries. His London School of Business MBA was as good as gold because it wouldn't be verified, and he was using his own name and tax identification, so he was free and clear. He was back in the game in a bigger way than ever before. But just to make sure he stayed on top, he figured he'd better try to stay as legitimate as he could. He was paranoid that somebody in the office would discover that his London School of Business MBA was completely without academic merit. So on his company CV – the copy that was circulated through the office – he made a slight modification and changed his Master's degree to one from the London School of Economics.

With that one word change – "Business" to "Economics" – he was suddenly an instant expert on anything business-related. It was a real school, after all, whereas the degree he'd purchased had come from a school that didn't actually exist. And because this new educational credential was a foreign degree, there was no need to worry that it would get caught in any verification process. Once again, things were falling into place way too easily for John Falcetta. He was now free to talk about his expertise garnered from years spent learning at the feet of the financial wizards housed in the London School of Economics. The whole scheme was, to John's mind, so brilliant it would impress even the British.

He stayed with Mercer for a few years, and nobody questioned anything on any of his credentials. It was all locked away in his personal file, safe and sound. But as luck would have it, he happened to run into a few guys who'd gone to the London School of Economics. And these guys had gone for real.

Once upon a time, a meeting like this could have proven disastrous to John, but he'd learned from his past mistakes and he'd paid a visit to see some family members in the United Kingdom. And while he was there, he'd gone on a tour of the London School of Economics. So when confronted with a situation where he had to be able to talk about his time there – like over drinks with colleagues who were alumni – he was able to talk about buildings, professors, the scenery, whatever. As a result, when they started talking about Sir John Hicks and his Nobel Prize or about late nights in the Main Library in the Lionel Robbins Building, he was like a fish in water. Nobody suspected a thing. The ultimate test came when one of the chief officers of the firm called him up to his office. At first John thought he was caught. But it turned out that he, too, had gone to LSE, and wanted to shoot the shit about old times. John pulled it off, and at that point he knew that he could fool anybody. And given that he was bringing in over $2 million annually for the company, they weren't too inclined to ferret him out.

But through all the lies and all the deception, at the end of the day, there was one thing that John couldn't fake: his work ethic. There was no amount of subterfuge he could employ that would make others think he was a better employee than he was. But the fact of the matter was that he didn't need any kind of dishonesty in that. Whether it was his clients or his bosses or his co-workers, everyone knew of John's commitment to the firm, his loyalty and his devotion. It was almost superhuman. And it wasn't just at Mercer. The team at Merrill had seen it, as had everyone at Paine Webber. John Falcetta, for all of his shortcomings, was the real deal when it came down to getting the job done. And nobody could deny that, no matter what they thought of John.

It's been said that success breeds confidence, and that confidence breeds success. And given his successes with the game to this point, John was gaining more and more confidence every day. He was content with his current situation, but wondered if there wasn't something else out there, something more lucrative. After all, the grass is always greener, right? And that three-headed monster that is greed is always searching for its next meal. So John's desire for more money and responsibility paired with his growing confidence in this little scam was the perfect target for an email that circulated around the office at Mercer one morning, an email from a headhunter seeking to fill a position within a Mercer client's executive branch.

After a little digging, John learned that the job in question was running worldwide benefits for Campbell's Soup, a $200 million responsibility. This was major. Really major. The company had been searching for a year to fill the position, but to no avail. After five different interviewers told him five different things about what the company was looking for in the person who would fill this job, John finally ended up sitting across a desk from Ed Walsh, Senior Vice President of Human Resources. Ed was known for his take-no-prisoners and accept-no-bullshit method of approaching things. He was a Princeton man, and whatever they'd taught him there, the United States Marine Corps had sharpened. This was David versus Goliath. Walsh stared at John, John stared right back. After a few minutes, Ed asked John what he thought of the job.

"Ed," he began, "as a consultant who bills clients four-hundred-twenty-five-bucks an hour, I suggest you listen to what I have to say very carefully. The reason this job is still open is because your own staff doesn't have a clue what the job is or what it's supposed to do. You should end this search now and not waste anyone's time until you get it all sorted out. Now, speaking as a candidate, from what I've heard so far, you need a comprehensive global health-care strategy that addresses long-term cost trends and quality of care. And that's just for starters."

He paused for breath and let his tirade hang there in the air for a second. David had nailed Goliath right between the eyes with a big rock. The two men sat silently for a few endless seconds, both staring at one another. Finally Walsh blinked and picked up the legal pad that was sitting on his desk.

"What are you making now?" he asked John.

Inside, John could feel his blood pressure spiking from excitement. The rookie ballplayer had just taken Nolan Ryan out of the park on his first swing. But he managed to keep his poise long enough to do a little more selling. He'd done his homework prior to this interview, and he knew that Campbell's compensated on a four-level system: base salary, bonus, stock options and long-term plan. So John took the legal pad from Walsh and wrote down his answer: "155, +, +, +."

Walsh looked down at the legal pad that John that pushed across the desk to him, raised an eyebrow slightly and looked back up at John. "What do the plusses look like?" he asked.

John didn't bat an eyelash. "One-fifty-five, a forty percent bonus and give-or-take a hundred thousand on the other two."

With that, Ed Walsh stood, extended his hand to John and thanked him for his time. He asked John to say hello to his colleagues at Mercer, which John assured him he would do. The interview had come to an abrupt end. John looked at his watch. It was five minutes before four o'clock in the afternoon.

By the time he'd driven home to Baltimore that evening, there was an offer from Campbell's waiting for him. The total compensation of the offer came in at around $325,000 annually. Not too shabby for a guy that had gotten kicked out of college before the end of his sophomore year. Not too shabby at all.

*   *   *

In his new position, John was a Global Director, meaning he was part of the senior management team at Campbell's, one of the top 200 employees out of a workforce of 35,000. One of the perks of that title was that he controlled jobs, some vendors, consultants and contractors. He had it in his power to ensure that he would never be found out for the lies that he used, simply because if anybody who looked like they could blow his cover happened along, he would deny them entrance to the kingdom. Life as the gatekeeper was good. He regularly quizzed staff members about HR procedures and compared notes with colleagues in similar positions at other firms to find out how their policies differed from those at Campbell's. He absorbed information like a sponge, making mental notes the whole time about what he could and couldn't get away with, should he ever need that sort of information in the future.

In other words, he was refining his scam. Just like a petty thief in prison, he was perfecting his techniques, waiting for his chance to pull off the big one, the one that he'd look back on as the one that made him famous. Or maybe it was just that he knew – like all scam artists do – that one day he'd get caught and he'd need to be able to pull another similar scam with another company one day. Either way, he took in and processed as much information as he could to ensure that when the opportunity – or the necessity – arose, he'd be ready.

It wasn't all a game to John, that much needs to be understood. He had a gyrating moral compass beneath his façade of hardened businessman. He understood the gravity of what it was he was doing, and he understood that he was doing explicitly illegal things. But he justified it in his own mind by exerting extra effort once hired, by working those twenty-hour days that impressed his co-workers. He felt that his results made up for a few little white lies, and nobody in the company seemed inclined to argue with the results he produced.

At this point in time, John thought he was getting pretty good at this little game of playing grown-up-in-corporate-America. He was respected at work, he was making a lot of money, he had the authority that he had longed for. He made more than a few enemies within the company, due in no small part to his acting as a voice of change, trying to streamline operations and manage costs and create value, but that was to be expected. When you're talking about a company that's been around since 1869, you don't come in barking about how things need to change in order for the company to become more profitable. It's just not the way it's done. But that's just how John was. If he saw something that needed improvement, he voiced his opinion. He constantly sought to streamline operations, to make a company more profitable. Arguments about change aside, all in all, John settled in to his role quite nicely and had accepted his position as a wannabe-mover-and-shaker – if not an effecter of change – and was content with his new station in life.

But then came the day, as it always seemed to do, when something went drastically wrong. John got a call from the Payroll department some time late in January the first year after he'd started working. They were issuing W-2s, and his Social Security number had bounced back as an invalid number. He hastily sent them an email with the correct Social Security number – the one that included his bankruptcy and his arrest – and crossed his fingers. Because the new-hire process was over and he'd been officially brought on as an employee, he hoped the number wouldn't be vetted in the same way as it would have been for a prospective employee.

At this point, he wasn't too worried about it, because one thing he'd learned in his time working in corporate America was that different departments didn't talk to each other. The Payroll department folks couldn't care less what the gang in Human Resources was doing, and both of them couldn't give two squirts about what the clowns in Marketing were doing. All the guys in Payroll wanted was a valid Social Security number; they didn't care what kind of information might be attached to it. That was Human Resources' concern, and since John himself was in Human Resources, it was his own concern that he would deal with as he saw fit. Long story short, what could have been a huge problem for him ended up being no problem at all.

In an odd twist, however, it wasn't John's history that caught up with him, but rather his attitude. After two years of listening to the new kid in the company call for change, Ed Walsh, together with a couple of John's superiors at Campbell's, had John bounced out. Yet again John was labeled a "disruptive influence," and once again he found himself out of a job. Ironically enough, it was a few days after his dismissal from Campbell's that the company auditors discovered that John's global healthcare initiative had saved the company millions of dollars and had vastly improved the health insurance benefits for Campbell's retirees.

After his dismissal from Campbell's, John got a phone call from an old friend from his days at Merrill Lynch. The friend had no idea about any of the events in John's past — nothing about the arrest, nothing about the bankruptcy, nothing about his less-than-noble departure from Wall Street — and he wanted to talk to John about a job. He and a couple of the brokers that had worked together at Merrill with John were running a pretty major Wall Street subsidiary for Lehman Brothers, and they were looking for somebody to be their number one Human Resources guy at a private equity deal they were doing with Monsanto and Hercules. They'd heard great things about his work. Would John be interested in the job?

He considered the offer for all of about ten seconds before jumping at it. They asked him for zero documentation. Not a single piece of paper. They just figured that what they knew of him was enough, especially when that personal background was paired with his recent tenure at Campbell's. So all of a sudden, John Falcetta found himself in the first quasi-honestly-acquired position he'd ever held. Because they hadn't asked him for anything, he hadn't been forced to give them any false information. To his mind — which, admittedly, was a little twisted at that point — it was a conscience-cleansing moment. For the first time in his professional life, he hadn't had to directly lie to his employer to get his job.

Yet again, everything was going smoothly. By now, John truly felt like he could stay where he was for as long as he wanted. He'd earned the complete trust of everyone he worked for, and there was no reason to think that anybody would ever come along to question his integrity. He was using his own name and his own tax information, so it wasn't like somebody could knock on the door and say that he was a fraud because somebody with the same name was a client of the firm's. And what's more, John was in charge of hiring, so he could filter out anybody who might even get a whiff of the fact that he had a checkered past. John took a deep breath, hit the clutch and shifted into fifth, letting the road unfold before him as he sat back and enjoyed the ride. During his time there, he managed to triple the company's value, which helped secure a multi-million dollar payout for John.

But it all came to a screeching halt when the company got sold. It was a recurring theme in his life to this point. Just when things seemed like they'd settled into a comfortable position, an earthquake came along and jostled everything around, making it all a big mess again. John was given a severance package and sent out into the world again to search for yet another job.

He'd taken his game to the highest level yet, and the confidence that he'd built up had convinced him that there wasn't a corporation on the planet that he couldn't fool. He'd been on the inside of the Human Resources office, so he knew the ins and outs. He knew how far he could push it and when he needed to pull back. He knew how to beat the background checks and how to talk the talk that would get him hired. He felt invincible. He'd developed an encyclopedic knowledge of systems, processes and procedures. But most of all, he'd become the skilled executive he'd always thought of his father as. He'd achieved greatness and was ready for more. The big fish had outgrown the small pond, so it was time to move on.

And that was his thinking when he spoke to a corporate headhunter about submitting his résumé to American International Group, the company most people know simply by its initials: AIG. This would be the ultimate test for the general, the battle that would either earn him that elusive fifth star or send him out in a body bag. As the Spartan wives used to say to their husbands as they headed out into battle, *aut cum scuto aut in scuto*. Either come in carrying your shield or on your shield. Either come home alive or dead.

John Falcetta, the battle-tested soldier, planned to come back carrying his shield, no matter how much blood stained it.

CHAPTER TWO
Mistaken Identity

Despite the fact that he'd lived his professional life to this point going from one con game to another, John Falcetta had managed to make some decent contacts in the upper echelons of the business world, and a lot of those people thought very highly of his abilities. In January of 2005, John was contacted by Ron Cole, a corporate headhunter. Cole was seeking to fill a position on behalf of one of his corporate clients; he didn't tell John who the company was at first, but assured him that it was an upper-level position with a major New York firm. He explained that the firm in question was looking for a new Vice President within its Human Resources department, and the position paid five hundred thousand dollars a year, with incentive bonuses built in to the contract. Far from chump change to be sure. John had a momentary vision of the man he'd met in the bar in New York, the one who'd started him on his path of fraud and deception.

John met with Cole and the two spoke about the position; at that point, Ron told John that the company in question was AIG. They talked about John's work experience for an hour or so, and Ron was overtly unimpressed. He actually told John that he felt that AIG had identified a better candidate — an internal candidate — and, because it was his professional obligation to recommend the best candidate for the position, he would be recommending that they hire that candidate over John. The two men parted ways, and John's spirits sank. He returned home and, during the next few months, pored over job listings on the Internet, but turned up nothing of interest.

Five months later, his phone rang. It was Ron Cole again. The internal candidate that Ron had been favoring for the position had declined the position; apparently the guy didn't want to move to New York City, regardless of the pay and benefits. Ron then went for his second choice, John Falcetta. And with that, John was right back in the running. Right back in the game.

But he didn't jump in with quite as much vigor as he'd thought he would. This newest revelation created a web of mixed emotions in John's mind, as he'd already wrapped his mind around the fact that he wasn't going to be hired by AIG. But now that he stood a good chance, the old butterflies started welling up in his stomach again. On the one hand, they were talking about a phenomenal amount of money, which was immensely gratifying and exciting. On the other hand, however, he was nervous to an equal degree, because he was sure that the people who would be vetting his application were going to be sophisticated. Very sophisticated, in fact. He had to remind himself that AIG is one of the world's biggest employers, with employees in more than 130 countries. But once again, John figured that he had nothing to lose and everything to gain, sophistication be damned. So once more into the breaches he launched himself, and sent in the standard package of lies, with a little bit of extra embellishment thrown in for good measure.

He modified the old scheme to make things seem a little more legitimate, a ploy he thought would be the best way to circumvent the background checks they'd be employing. He used his father's Social Security number and college credentials, which would ensure that when they checked it out, his name would match and his record would be clean. If they wanted to call the school, they'd be happy to tell them that yes, in fact, John Falcetta had attended and graduated. If they ran a credit check, they'd find that, yes indeed, John Falcetta had a clean credit rating. He paired that information with his purchased London School of Business MBA, which he could at least produce as proof that he had a diploma.

All of that fake education he supplemented with his experiences at Merrill Lynch, a smattering of financial groups and his time at Campbell's Soup. But he couldn't very well mention the work experience from when he was living life as somebody else and working at Paine Webber, so he had to create a few jobs that were relevant enough to the job he was applying for, as well as to fill in the chronological gap from his days living and working then. He made sure to keep the names he was using for his fictional work experience obscure enough so as to avoid the risk of running into someone else who'd actually worked at those firms, but still big enough to lend some credibility. It helped, too, that he picked companies who had long since merged with other firms, so his fake experiences with them would be even more difficult to verify. He was simply trying to fill in gaps of time. He never invented work experiences that he didn't have. He merely exaggerated some things here and there and made up a few details as he felt he needed to. The experiences were legitimate; the timing may have been slightly off. He saw it as minor deviation from the truth and nothing more.

Once the application and relevant materials had been sent in, John just crossed his fingers and hoped that nobody would look too closely. He was relying on what he'd learned as an HR exec to manipulate the system. He was banking on the fact that AIG's Human Resources department worked much like any other HR department in terms of how and what they would investigate. He hoped they wouldn't see fit to verify overseas degrees and that they wouldn't work too hard to look at things like when he supposedly graduated from college. His only chance at success here lay in his hunch that HR departments were more or less the same all over the world. If he guessed wrong, however, they'd have an easy enough time spotting him as the fraud that he was. Roll the dice and pray for a seven.

John met one last time with the head of HR from AIG. He was told it was a formality, that they just wanted to make sure everything was signed, sealed and delivered. It was a brief meeting, thirty minutes at most. At the conclusion, he stood and shook hands with his interviewer. John was told it would take a few days to fully vet his credentials, but that assuming everything checked out (and there was no reason that it shouldn't, right? wink, wink, nudge, nudge), he could expect an offer soon after they'd finished the background check.

John went home from that meeting again unsure of what to think. He was working hard not to get his hopes too high, but it was tough to keep them in check. He swore to himself that this was the last one – if he got this job, he was done with the frauds. He was like a drunk hunched over the toilet at the end of a long night, making promises to God, to the devil, to whomever happened to be listening at a given moment. Just let me get away with it this one last time, and I swear no more. And I really mean it this time.

Because he was hoping for an offer and because he didn't want to run the risk of getting caught again – and besides, he'd also made that promise to the powers-that-be about stopping his lies – he didn't seek out any additional job leads in the event AIG declined to offer. Instead he focused his attention on that megalith that he hoped he'd been able to con one last time into offering him a position. And when you're unemployed and waiting for an offer, you've got a lot of time to do research.

*   *   *

American International Group was founded in 1919 by Cornelius Vander Starr. The ironic thing about the company's founding, at least given the name Starr chose, is that AIG's first office was in Shanghai, China. Starr called his new venture American Asiatic Underwriters, and focused on selling personal insurance policies to the Chinese. His business flourished until 1949, when Mao Zedong led his Communist-affiliated People's Liberation Army against the Kuomintang in the Chinese Civil War. When the Communists seized control, Starr moved his operations west, to New York City. And thus American Asiatic Underwriters became American International Group.

Maurice Greenberg – "Hank" to everyone besides his mother – took over management of AIG in 1962. Six years later, Greenberg took over the reins of AIG from Starr, and in 1969 the company went public. Greenberg took the company in a new direction – he went from using agents to sell insurance to independent brokers in order to save the company the agents' salaries, and he shifted the corporate focus from selling personal insurance policies to more lucrative corporate coverage policies. The change in strategy worked, as AIG quickly became one of the world's largest companies. Its stock was included as a part of the Dow Jones Industrial Average beginning in 2004 (though it was removed in September of 2008). The company is routinely listed as one of the world's largest twenty companies, with offices in North America, Europe, the United Kingdom, Indonesia, Australia, India, Pakistan, the Philippines and Asia, as well as a smattering of Latin American countries.

In the United States, AIG is the largest underwriter of commercial and industrial insurance; American General, an AIG subsidiary, is one of the nation's largest providers of life insurance policies. AIG Direct, another AIG subsidiary, is a major writer of automotive insurance policies throughout the United States. AIG's holdings include insurance companies worldwide, as well as financial service companies and asset management firms. And other holdings of the firm include the Stowe Mountain ski resort in Stowe, Vermont; the Bulgarian Telecommunications Company in Sofia, Bulgaria; Lincoln Property Company in Dallas, Texas; and International Lease Finance Corporation, the world's largest aerospace leasing agency, located in Los Angeles, California. All told, AIG owns, at least in part, over a hundred different subsidiary companies spread out over more than 130 countries, employing over 115,000 people.

And with a little luck, John Falcetta would be able to join the ranks of those 115,000.

*   *   *

John's phone rang some time in late August of 2005. A young female voice with a distinctly Southern accent asked to speak with John Falcetta. When John identified himself as the man she was looking for, she said that she was calling from a firm in Texas who had been hired by AIG to do background checks on prospective employees. She had a few questions about his application, as there had been some flags raised. Specifically, she said, there was an issue with multiple Social Security numbers. John's heart sank. He figured this was the part where his hopes of half-a-million dollars annually flew out the window.

As it turned out, a former employer had let slip the fact that the background checker had the wrong Social Security number. And they were helpful enough to give her the correct one – or at least the one they had on file. That was the bad news. The good news was that the two Social Security numbers they had were clean – neither showed John's arrest record or his bankruptcy. The one he'd provided himself was his father's, which was clean; the other, provided by the former employer, was his federal tax identification number. But he was stuck.

John thought fast and, figuring it was all or nothing, threw a grenade on the fire. "They must have given you the wrong information," he said firmly. "I've obviously never had more than one Social Security number, so I don't know where they got it from. Who was the employer that gave you the number anyway?"

She wouldn't answer, but apparently accepted his explanation as viable enough to be true. She wasn't getting paid enough to cross-examine applicants, so she moved on to the next point that needed clarification, namely the arrest record for a guy named John Falcetta back in 1989. She asked point-blank if John had ever been arrested before.

"Absolutely not," he said, trying to sound as if he'd just heard the funniest thing anyone had said all day and yet he was still a little offended by the humor.

"You're sure you were never arrested in New York?"

Again John asserted his innocence. "Why are you asking me this?" He knew damn well why she was asking, but he was trying to sound confused and irritated, because he felt cornered.

The girl on the other end of the phone didn't answer. "What about bankruptcy?" she asked. "Have you ever declared bankruptcy?"

It was obvious this woman had found the information John had been hiding from for over ten years. She was good, that was for sure, but she wasn't Perry Mason. She wasn't going to get him to admit to something he didn't want to admit to. He took a deep breath and began. "No. Never. I've never declared bankruptcy. I've never been arrested. Now, please tell me why you're asking me these questions." He was sounding increasingly forceful, like a man who was utterly above this asinine behavior and who was growing tired of being asked such menial questions.

Finally the voice on the other end relaxed slightly. "You're not going to believe this, Mr. Falcetta, but there's a man with your same name and same approximate age who's been raising all kinds of Hell in New York. First he declared bankruptcy, and then he got arrested for attempted theft by check, but got off with probation. All this was back in nineteen-eighty-nine." She laughed slightly.

"I never lived in New York," John managed to say.

The sound of shuffling papers came across the line underneath the sound of her voice. "In that case, it must have been someone else. Thanks for your time, Mr. Falcetta. I'm glad everything checked out." She hung up. And that was it. He couldn't have imagined it being any easier. All of the butterflies and all of the worry had been, for all intents and purposes, for no reason at all.

The next day, John received another call, this time from the HR department at AIG. They were offering him the job of Vice President of Human Resources within AIG Life. He would be overseeing a division with approximately $60 billion in annual revenue. He would have 40,000 employees under him worldwide, with a personal staff of nine in New York City alone and three hundred additional staffers globally. Cumulatively this group would make somewhere in the neighborhood of $1 billion annually before bonuses. It was a massive responsibility, and he would be compensated accordingly. Was he interested?

You bet your ass he was interested. And more importantly, he'd done it. He'd gotten past the mighty AIG screening system and was now teetering on the edge of his wildest dreams becoming reality. Just maybe he had overestimated these guys. Just maybe they weren't quite as sophisticated as he had thought they were. After all, he'd scammed them pretty easily.

He was good, there was no question about it. He'd skirted his way around what was, arguably, one of the most complex background checks in the American business world. But getting past the barrier and into the position was one thing. Staying there would be another thing altogether, and it was going to take just as much creativity – not to mention luck – for John to keep his place.

"The income tax has made more liars out of the
American people than golf has."
—Will Rogers

CHAPTER THREE
An Open Checkbook

John, in what had by now become an all-too-familiar pattern, settled into his new role as Vice President of Human Resources in AIG's Worldwide Life Insurance division, whose largest subsidiary is American Life Insurance Company (ALICO). It was the typical Falcetta situation – he had lied to get the position, but once in it, he gave it his all and accomplished things that would usually only be attributed to people with the qualifications he claimed to have. John didn't have it in him to work at a job without performing his duties to exemplary levels; his fraudulent activities that got him kicked out of the ROTC program in college notwithstanding, John Falcetta would have made one hell of a soldier. He found new and better ways to do old things. He did what he was told and he did it without question. And what's more, he did it better than anybody else around him.

Perhaps that was the quality that landed him the job at AIG in the first place, because you have to believe that those who had the final say in his hiring knew what he was going to be asked to do. And to get done what they wanted to get done, they'd need somebody who did exactly what he was told without asking any questions. John had been interviewed by a host of AIG executives – including AIG's CEO Martin Sullivan, AIG's Senior Vice Chairman Edmund Tse, AIG's COO Donald Kanak, ALICO's CEO Ken Nottingham and many others – and they'd all approved his application. Was his alma mater really that important? Was a financial decision nearly two decades earlier reason to pass on what might be their dream employee?

The American Life Insurance Company was chartered in 1921 in

Delaware. Delaware is one of two states in the United States – Nevada is the other one – that is a haven for American corporations seeking to legitimately minimize state tax liability in the states where they operate. In the case of ALICO, they operated under the AIG corporate umbrella that covers all of the components of what is a New York-based holding company. By having the company chartered in Delaware as opposed to its home state of New York, however, AIG could avoid paying New York state taxes. But why Delaware of all places?

Delaware has long been known as the next best thing to an offshore bank account in terms of avoiding paying taxes. A *New York Times* article from May 29, 2009, referred to Delaware as an "onshore refuge" for those seeking the benefits of offshore accounts closer to home. The tax codes are complex, and just like any other processes, the more steps involved, the more complex they get.

The simplest way to look at is to think of a holding company as the parent and its Delaware subsidiary (or subsidiaries, as the case may be) as children. So a big holding company – like AIG – opens up a "shell" company in Delaware. That shell typically doesn't have an actual office that employs anybody in the traditional sense, but rather just serves as a mailing address. So AIG, headquartered in New York City, sets up the American Life Insurance Company shell, with "headquarters" in Delaware. The AIG parents then give their child ownership of all assets they acquire as a result of ALICO's business. So the shell is something of a depository in that sense. All of that income that the shell takes in is, by Delaware law, not taxed by the state.

Now, a company like AIG is actually in the business of making money, and if they just give away all of their profits to these shell companies, they're not going to be making money, right? So they, in turn, get loans from their shell companies, loans that the shells are more than willing to make. And because the loan itself isn't income per se, it's not taxable income, at least according to the IRS. So in a twist that only parents can truly appreciate, the metaphorical child loans money to the parent, money that was originally the parent's, but which the parent had sent to the child. This whole set-up gives a whole new meaning to the idea of a shell game.

AIG, however, is certainly not alone in their desire to avoid paying taxes, nor are they alone in their use of Delaware holding companies to assist in the avoidance of paying those taxes. There are some 6500 different such shell companies that are headquartered on one street alone in Wilmington, Delaware. Or, more specifically, at least 6500 companies that exist on paper are headquartered there. Whether or not they employ anybody is another matter.

John's job at AIG had begun in September, 2005, and for a period of a few months, he learned the ins and outs of life as an executive at AIG. He enjoyed a few of the perks of his position – but use of the executive dining room, with white linen table cloths, the finest food and a staff of uniformed waiters to serve it, wasn't one of them. Despite the fact that all of the services offered in the most exclusives of the three dining rooms in the AIG Tower were free – after all, at his pay grade, he couldn't be expected to actually buy his own lunch, could he? – that just wasn't how John Falcetta rolled. At least not at that time. It always boggled his mind, however, that those who chose to dine there did so without the least thought of why the administrative staff was forced to eat in a different cafeteria – two floors below the Executive Dining Room – where the sneeze guard got cleaned off twice an hour and a salad was ten bucks. The Executive Dining Room is one of the grand hypocrisies of corporate America.

After his first month with AIG, John was approached by Kendall Nottingham, Chairman of ALICO. Ken was a former Navy man. He was a graduate of the Naval Academy, in fact; his office was even decorated with

Naval-themed artwork. He was a large man, bordering on rotund, with a great sense of humor. He'd been part of John's lengthy interview process, during which time John had made several mental notes that the man seemed like the true embodiment of an Anglophile. He loved to talk about his extravagant vacations — he was the sort of man who would tell you about his "Atlantic crossing aboard the Queen."

He was also something of a self-important task master who went so far as to assign himself two secretaries, just in case one or the other needed back-up during an especially time-consuming phone call. And the two secretaries themselves battled for superiority. If Ken wanted coffee, he would ask one of his secretaries to get it; she would, in turn, pass the task off to the other secretary, who would have nowhere to go but to the coffee maker. The message was that, despite the fact that the two women wielded equal authority, the one who had to get the coffee was deemed the lower ranking of the two.

Perhaps harkening back to his days in the Navy, Nottingham got a great deal of pleasure from watching fellow executives battle over issues within the company, always keeping himself above the fray and refusing to enter, even to serve as a moderator. He often displayed email or fax exchanges between his colleagues that he'd joke about, exchanges that would grow increasingly heated over the course of time. Passive aggressive behavior was one of Nottingham's other well-known characteristics.

When he approached John on that fateful morning, Nottingham had what was, on the surface, a relatively routine request. He asked John to work with his senior management team to find a way to continue making bonus payments. On the surface, when one reads that, it sounds as if ALICO was somehow running out of money and would not be able to pay their executives bonuses. While that would become the new reality by the end of 2008 — or at least it was the reality before the American taxpayers stepped in and saved them — during October, 2005, ALICO and AIG had plenty of money with which to pay salaries and bonuses and all the sorts of monetary issues that HR execs concern themselves with. But this request, despite its quotidian façade, was anything but ordinary.

This was the first time John learned of a "company" that AIG maintained specifically for the purpose of paying executives, with monies that were held in a Bermuda bank that few people within AIG knew existed. John was not told the specifics of how the company itself was used, and Nottingham left it at that, telling John to get in touch with Eric Rohtla, Vice President and Director of International Emerging Markets and Business Development for ALICO, and Bruce Dozier, Senior Vice President and General Counsel at ALICO. They would, Nottingham told him, instruct him on the operations of the Bermuda company, which was called AICO.

John knew both men. Rohtla — whose nickname was Rottweiler — was that kid in every class, the one who thinks he knows it all and doesn't stop talking about it. He'd been instrumental in opening up Eastern Europe as a location for AIG offices, and he'd been talking about it ever since. He was in his late forties, and he'd put in a lot of time over the course of those years at AIG. He'd worked himself ragged, too, helping to bring in billions of dollars for the firm. He was overworked and underpaid, but also one of those guys who'd talk to you at length about exactly that combination of unfortunate circumstances if you gave him half the chance. He was also notorious around the office for blaming the guy who wasn't in the room for whatever was going wrong at a given moment. It never failed. The guy who wasn't there was inevitably the guy who was "dragging his feet getting the paperwork finished" or the guy who was "refusing to call back until he gets all the numbers run."

Bruce was a horse of an entirely different color, at least to John's mind. He was a decent guy, a hardworking lawyer who reminded people of a college professor who was disliked by most with whom he worked. He was, at the time, going through a relatively contentious divorce and some serious health issues, both of which no doubt colored his perception of the world and, because of that, the image that others had of him. As the General Counsel of ALICO (a Delaware-based company) he was routinely having run-ins with the Delaware regulators, run-ins that, amazingly enough, always seemed to end in Bruce's favor.

Though John had no inkling at the time, he and Bruce were to become quite close during John's tenure at AIG, due to the fact that John was in the unfortunate position of having to clean up the mess that was left after Bruce's untimely dismissal from the company. At the age of fifty-nine – one year away from his multi-million-dollar AIG partner plan payout – Bruce was terminated, an order that came down from Edmund Tse and Rod Martin, the Chairman of ALICO.

Following the initial meeting with Nottingham, John was delivered a package from Rohtla, a package that contained materials related to the Bermuda company. But beyond a collection of bank statements and spreadsheets, there was little to explain what Falcetta was to do with the accounts in terms of bonus payments. It was, he assumed, something that would eventually be explained to him, and he went about his daily routine without focusing too much energy on the Bermuda entity.

Bermuda as a country has, over the years, achieved a status of "tax haven supreme" for those *über*-wealthy individuals with a need to hide massive amounts of money from federal taxation officials in America. Much the same descriptor has been applied to banks in other foreign lands, including Switzerland, the Cayman Islands and Singapore, to name only a few. What all of these account locations have in common is the fact that they don't report to the Internal Revenue Service, meaning the amount you have in that account is between you and the bank. Nor do they report to the IRS equivalents in the foreign countries where AIG does business.

On the surface, there are arguments about how an offshore account can help protect your assets from liability. In reality, though, the accounts are all about avoiding taxes; in reality, a Bermuda bank account was just an external manifestation of greed. In the case of AIG, the Bermuda entity was a manifestation of corporate greed. And this was John's baptism into the culture of corporate greed that dominated the inner workings of AIG.

John knew that a secret Bermuda account maintained or used by a US corporation that has the size and sophistication of AIG – especially a Bermuda account that few people within the firm even knew existed – had the potential to be that much more dangerous. He hadn't signed on for this, no matter how much of a fraud his résumé might have been. He worked very hard to put the whole thing in a sort of mental strongbox, somewhere in his brain that those thoughts about the offshore account wouldn't dominate his thinking. Somewhere he could hide them. Or at least hide from them.

The following month, however, the issue was brought to the forefront for John. At the beginning of November, Nottingham summoned John to his office and instructed him to issue a check in the amount of $50,000 for Marc Sevestre, the President of ALICO's western Europe branch. The check was not to be processed through the French Human Resources office as would be the customary way of handling such payments in the European office; rather, it was to be drawn on the Bermuda account. And John's signature would be on the approval.

What Mr. Sevestre chose to do in terms of reporting the check as income was his own business. But because it would be drawn on the Bermuda account, there would be no record of it as having come from AIG. Additionally, the payment would by-pass the established rules and regulations, including corporate compliance for tax and reporting purposes. The only exception to that lack of a record would be if Sevestre voluntarily chose to report the income. In other words, Sevestre was under a legal obligation to report the income; but if he chose not to, there would be no record of it with the French tax authorities.

John did not know and could not have known whether Sevestre opted to report the payments in his tax returns or whether he was required by applicable law to make such disclosure and pay tax. If Sevestre chose to report the income, the matter ends at that point as far as it concerns Sevestre. Why AIG would elect to make payments to an employee through a Bermuda account in a situation where the employee reports the receipt of income and pays tax thereon was not something that was readily apparent to John, nor did he choose to investigate it. The whole operation was, frankly, Sevestre's business not John's, and John did not need to concern himself with the decision ultimately made by Sevestre.

And even though it wasn't his business to be worrying about it – he had been hired to be a good (and well-paid) foot soldier, not a living manifestation of somebody's conscience – John knew in the back of his mind that payment of executives working in various different countries for different subsidiaries of AIG through a Bermuda entity was not within the normal sphere of established corporate compensation policy, but he lacked the immediate resources to confirm the specific legalities involved.

John's mind flashed back for a moment to his days as the seven-year-old kid who was too smart for his own good, the one that got stuffed into trash cans by jealous peers that mercilessly attacked him for his skills in the classroom that made the rest of them look less intelligent. Maybe this was something similar, a big joke they played on the new kid to see how far he'd really go for the company. Was he willing to deviate from the expected and normal compensation practice of AIG which had built-in accounting and reporting functionality in favor of an unorthodox payment structure outside the established norms? Maybe this was an in-house test of his loyalties to make sure he was a real team player? He could only hope that was the case, because if he was really being asked to conspire to abet international income tax evasion, that might just be a bigger scam than even he was ready to perpetrate.

John went to the man who was, for all intents and purposes, his mentor at AIG, Tom Hoffman, the man whom John was replacing as Vice President of Human Resources. Hoffman was still in the office, gradually phasing himself into retirement and allowing John to look over his shoulder – while simultaneously looking over John's shoulder – so that Falcetta could learn the specifics of the job first-hand. The two had an amiable relationship. They shared a similar sense of humor and similar work ethics. So when John went to him with a question that he wasn't entirely sure was a serious request, he halfway expected Hoffman to slap him on the back and laugh loudly, telling him that it was all a big joke and welcome to the club.

But when John asked Hoffman about the Bermuda payment scheme, the answer he got was completely devoid of humor. The two sat in Hoffman's office as Hoffman explained the specifics of how AIG used the Bermuda company to provide specific types of payments to some of its executives. This wasn't an account that was used for everybody, Hoffman explained. Only those above a certain pay grade who had the explicit trust of Edmund Tse. And it was only to be used for specific sorts of payments. For example, an executive who might be making $750,000 annually per his contract might get a portion of that salary through the HR department in his home country.

For example, an executive who might be making $750,000 annually per his contract might get a portion of that salary through the HR department in his home country. The remainder would come from the Bermuda account. He called it "split payroll."

He explained it to John like this: "Take that guy making seven-fifty. He might take six-hundred-thousand of it through the French company's payroll system, which leaves him short a hundred-fifty-thousand dollars." So here comes the guy with "the Bermuda checkbook" – and John Falcetta was now the guy with that checkbook – to make up the difference. The same held true for certain bonus payments, like the one John was being asked to pay to Marc Sevestre. And in the event any special needs arose – special needs that required somewhat secretive payments – the Bermuda account came to the rescue.

Of course this was unusual; it avoided the normal compensation procedures for purposes of reporting (both on a financial statement basis as well as for various tax laws). Depending on the nature of the employment (i.e., whether the employee actually rendered services for the Bermuda entity making the payment) and the tax laws of the country of the recipient's residence or citizenship, both the corporation making the payment as well as the recipient could be required to comply with a number of obligations, not the least of which would be that the recipient declare the income and pay tax in the relevant country if tax was imposed on foreign source earnings. And given that AIG had offices in over 130 countries that employed over 100,000 individuals, there was no telling whether AIG sought (or complied with) appropriate tax advice in each jurisdiction.

All the scams he'd run in the past – the Boy Scout uniform, the care packages at the University of Rochester, the fake degrees, the insurance policies – were nothing compared to what he felt he was being asked to do now. And the magnitude of the situation gave him pause; as he'd told himself many times before, this was a door that, once opened, couldn't be closed again. Once he took the first step and issued the first check off the Bermuda account, he'd have blood on his hands. And it would be his own blood.

According to federal tax laws in the United States and many other countries that AIG operates in, any taxpaying entity may take advantage of allowable means to minimize tax obligations. What that means, for example, is that an individual or a corporation can do things like make charitable donations to avoid paying taxes on income or select a variety of legally allowable means to defer income from one year to the next.

The key word in that whole description above is "allowable." Section 7201 of the Internal Revenue Code makes it a federal crime to "willfully attempt to evade or defeat the payment of federal income taxes." So doing things like hiding income or failing to report income are not allowed under the tax code. In other words, payment of compensation through a foreign financial entity by a US employer to a US employee rendering services wholly within the US would be deemed income tax evasion if the payment is designed to avoid compliance with reporting procedures specified by the Internal Revenue Code. John did not know at the time whether French law imposed similar obligations, but this would become known as events unfolded.

Of course, how AIG came to be in possession of the assets in the Bermuda account, or why compensation would be paid outside of the established payroll system of a publicly held corporation — especially a corporation that is allegedly subject to a series of audit procedures intended to provide safeguards for reporting of income and expenses, not to mention disclosure under securities laws in the US — was a topic for another discussion, one to which John Falcetta was not privy.

The Internal Revenue Code further outlines the basis for guilt of tax evasion in two parts. First, the evader must have substantial income that is not reported; "substantial" is an ambiguous term at best. Second, the taxpayer must knowingly and willingly attempt to evade paying the tax he would have been otherwise liable for. The word "attempted" in legalese indicates that the perpetrator of the act understood what he was doing in that he knew that he was avoiding tax payments by hiding income. It's all pretty cut-and-dried, especially when you're talking about people who are executives at a major international financial corporation – a major international financial corporation that in any event, and at least for its US employees rendering services in the US, is subject to mandatory withholding of tax at the source (for which the corporation must account to the IRS on an annual basis with a statement of income paid to the taxpayer) and a system which requires the employee to file tax returns (and estimated tax returns in the US) and pay tax on income received regardless of the withholding system. The same type of withholding and reporting rules are generally applied in most countries such as France. So it should have been common knowledge to a group of international finance experts that the laws in France, though the specific language might have been different, were much the same in spirit as they were in America.

In other words, these guys knew better. A lot better.

Here was life imitating art; it reminded him of a scene straight out of a John Grisham novel. A main character is invited into a job and then gradually sullied through illegal activities that the firm is engaged in, and because he's now a part of it, he's just as guilty as they are. The only thing was, he couldn't just dog ear a page and close the book, turn off the light and go to bed and leave it all behind. This was his life.

And they had him by the short hairs, didn't they? After all, what was he going to do? Tell them he'd suddenly developed an aversion to dishonest business practices? He'd have a tough time selling them on that, especially if they decided to do a little digging into his background and discovered everything the background check had missed. For the first time in his professional life, John Falcetta had run up against a scam that was bigger than anything he could fathom. He knew what happened to guys who didn't "play ball," guys who weren't "team players." Those were the guys who suddenly decided to "pursue other opportunities" at other companies.

John still held out hope that he could find a way out of this, somehow find out that this whole thing had been nothing but a big misunderstanding. So he approached Alex Grabcheski, a low-ranking Human Resources generalist who had spent years working with both Hoffman and Nottingham. Alex was well-known at AIG for his morning walk to work. Every morning that it wasn't raining, Alex would hike his way across the Brooklyn Bridge from his home in the neighborhood of Cobble Hill in Brooklyn. He was the kind of guy who would leave a suit jacket on the back of his chair at his desk while he went out. Anybody who didn't know better would see that jacket and think he'd just stepped out. If they actually took the time to wait for him, they'd realize he was gone for the day. Some days he'd leave at six. Some days he'd leave at noon. But that suit coat was always right there on that chair.

Because Grabcheski focused on practicality more than the underlying ethics and morality of situations that confronted him the idea of a payment made by a US corporation from a secret Bermuda payroll operation apparently was not something that burdened him. He laughed when John explained to him that he'd been asked to make what John thought was an extraordinary payment through the company's Bermuda entity.

"Bermuda's like an open checkbook that we use to solve problems," Grabcheski explained to him. John realized that it was the second time in as many conversations that he'd heard almost verbatim the same description of the Bermuda account's usage. This was to become the party line about the Bermuda operation, the "open checkbook" that the company used to solve problems.

Then Grabcheski told John more about payroll arrangements that particular AIG executives benefitted from. Payroll, stocks, bonuses, all types of payments were often split up at the request of the specific executive who was being compensated. Once split, they could be deposited in various locations: Switzerland, Brazil, Germany, the Caymans, Dubai, Hong Kong, the globe was the limit. He told him all of this "in the strictest of confidence," of course. One of Grabcheski's guilty pleasures was gossiping. He loved to tell everyone the dirt in exchange for other dirt that he could leverage for still more dirt later on.

As 2005 drew to a close, John was still stalling on approving the check for Sevestre. While he wanted to give his job his best effort — as was his custom — he found himself hitting a brick wall with this one, a brick wall that wouldn't allow him to get past the idea that it seemed much more profound a violation than anything he'd done in the past. Nottingham and Sevestre continued to press him for the payment, and John continued to put them off. He knew on some level that Bermuda was only going to become a four-letter word in his own personal lexicon, but also that the issue could very well lead to his premature departure from AIG.

At about this time, Nottingham met again with John in an attempt to assuage his fears. He told John in no uncertain terms that he saw nothing wrong — in fact, nothing illegal, for that matter — in the use of the Bermuda entity as a way of paying salaries. It wasn't AIG's business to play the part of Big Brother in some kind of Orwellian world; he refused to accept the role of police officer who was making sure that his employees did what they were legally obligated to do by making sure they declared all of their income. After all, he argued, what was to say that any employee who would willingly use the Bermuda payments to dodge income taxes wouldn't find another way to do it if they were paid in the traditional method off the HR payroll account?

He showed John letter upon letter — a stack of which he'd kept in his personal files — that detailed a history of payments from the Bermuda company. "It's just a regular part of doing business," he told John in a voice that resembled that of a father teaching his son about the ways of the world. "It's how we've always done things around here." John, however, wasn't convinced. John was reminded of his days selling insurance, when something on paper was all a client needed to see in order to take it as gospel truth. It wasn't working for him in this case. He knew that every firm on Wall Street – not to mention the rest of the country – would be doing the same thing if it were even remotely legal.

Sensing that the firm's new foot soldier was hesitant to take the plunge where Bermuda was concerned, Nottingham put Rohtla and Dozier back on the case. While it is impossible to know his precise motives, it isn't too outlandish an assumption to think that by sending a Vice President and a Senior Vice President (who also happened to be the division's General Counsel), Nottingham hoped to overwhelm Falcetta with reassurances from the highest levels that this was not quite as unsavory a practice as Falcetta thought. The pair assured John, over the course of several conversations, that this practice had been going on for over thirty years, almost parroting exactly what Nottingham had told him in his conversation with John. In a sort of conspiratorial move, however, they drew John into their plot in a way Nottingham didn't by suggesting that he could help them develop new ways to utilize the Bermuda payroll scheme because it could prove to be a sticky issue if the foreign tax authorities – or the IRS, for that matter – ever started nosing around too much.

The trio discussed such vehicles as split-employment contracts, consulting contracts and other ideas that could serve as ways to pay out tax-free bonuses off the Bermuda entity. All of it made John very uneasy; it was his name that would be on the signature line of those approvals, and it would all come right back to him if anybody decided to turn on him. At that point, Dozier told John a startling fact. Over forty ALICO executives were on the list of beneficiaries of the ongoing Bermuda payment scheme through such things as split-salary payments. While not somehow absolving him of any of the potential ramifications that could result from his involvement in this scheme, it was intriguing to hear that so many executives were, in essence, getting paid under the table. There was no reporting, no withholding, no W-2s, no 1099s, no documents. No paper trail. No way to prove they'd been paid the money and thus owed the income tax.

And on that list was John's own boss, Edmund Tse, the Senior Vice Chairman of AIG.

*   *   *

With the Christmas holiday approaching, thoughts around the Human Resources offices turned to bonuses. It was John's first Christmas in the office, so he was following Hoffman's lead. Hoffman told Falcetta that AIG didn't make it a priority to true-up their fourth quarter books with the overall budget, which is equivalent to not balancing your checkbook at the end of a statement period. "As long as there's an invoice," he explained, "nobody looks twice. So long as you don't go over budget, you're fine."

Hoffman made a few payments to vendors who, he explained to John, needed to be "kept happy" because they'd done a lot of work for no pay. The problem, in John's mind, was that there was no proof that these mysterious vendors had done any work at all; the only thing Hoffman had to go on was an invoice. There was no way anybody had of knowing whether or not these guys had done anything beyond watching TV all day, and John pointed that out to Hoffman. Hoffman winked at Falcetta as he repeated his explanation that nobody would look further at the payments, so long as there was an invoice. Just an invoice. Any invoice. Wink, wink, nudge, nudge.

John filed that fact in the back of his mind. John had no idea what these vendors had done for Hoffman in exchange for what looked like gratuitous payments, but he figured it could be valuable information one day. Just in case. To this day, he can't tell you exactly why he thought it was going to be important information to retain. Maybe it was because of the Bermuda issue, something that he knew in the back of his mind was going to haunt him for all of his days at AIG. Maybe it was because of the old adage about old dogs and new tricks. Whatever the reason, he remembered the fact that nobody in accounting would question a payment if an invoice was presented.

A few days later, John had lunch with an old friend, Tom Pombonyo. The pair met every year right before Christmas to have lunch at Sparks Steakhouse in midtown Manhattan, where they reminisced over old times and John toasted his good friend Brendan Dolan, who had worked and died in the World Trade Center in the terrorist attacks of September 11th. John lifted his glass of wine in memory of Brendan; Tom, as was his habit, toasted with club soda. Brendan had saved John's life many years earlier by reaching out to help him when they were both at the University of Rochester. It was an act of kindness that had kept John going and kept alive his belief in the inherent goodness of humanity. Brendan had kept alive in John the tiny spark of desire to keep on going.

Pombonyo is what is best described as "old school Italian." He was raised Catholic, but in a twist of fate that even Hollywood would have had trouble with, he converted to, of all things, Mormonism. Of course it was for a woman, so he at least had a reason behind his conversion. He embraced the Mormon faith as whole-heartedly as he had Catholicism, working his way up to the level of bishop within his local Mormon ward in Long Island. He and John had met in 1995, when Pombonyo was working as a corporate headhunter. Though he had done his fair share of work with major firms, these days he worked from home for the most part, selling insurance and doing some training and recruiting.

As it so often did, the talk eventually turned to work. John had just started working for AIG, and Pombonyo wanted to hear how things were going with his old friend. John was uncharacteristically reticent about the job itself, but his mind was working like mad, formulating and processing ideas. His friend sitting across the table from him was in a business that dovetailed perfectly with John's. John was in charge of hiring, and Tom was in charge of finding people that John could hire. As he sat there sipping his wine, John's brain spun together those two facts, and mixed in the conversation he'd had with Hoffman. And then slowly the gears clicked into place. John knew that with Tse's name on the "Bermuda list," there were going to be big problems for him, especially with Nottingham and Sevestre pressing him to authorize the payment. John saw his career at AIG ending quickly, and with the larceny in his heart well-rooted over the years, he only saw one safety net.

John looked across the table at Pombonyo and smiled ever so slightly. The old fire inside was beginning to grow. The scammer that John had sworn he'd never be again was starting to resurface, this time out of a combination of opportunity and panic. John went on to explain to Tom all that he'd learned about what he thought might be gratuitous payments to vendors – he elaborated both on the Bermuda scam and the end-of-year bonus payments that Hoffman was sending – and the fact that, so long as there was an invoice, AIG didn't look twice at the bills. At that point, Falcetta suggested that the two men see if they couldn't get paid for doing what amounted to marginal work at best.

It was like an alcoholic taking the first drink. He couldn't stop once he'd gotten started. No matter how good his intentions were going in, John found himself crawling back to the old behaviors. And once he'd gotten those old behaviors back in his mind, he was off and running.

Tom was hesitant. It was a risky operation. It was AIG, for God's sake.

There was no telling what they were capable of. But John reminded him that, as VP of Human Resources, he was in charge of approving head-hunting payments. John Falcetta was, in essence, the man with whom the buck stopped. If John approved it – and Tom could produce an invoice – there would be no problem at all. Results weren't important; documents were. AIG typically paid headhunters somewhere north of eighty-thousand dollars per successful hire. In other words, it was an incredibly lucrative contract for Tom, and with John's blessing covering the operation, Tom had nothing to worry about in terms of getting caught. This was, to John's mind, the perfect scam. He'd finally come across it. Like the Fountain of Youth or Shangri-La. Only this was the real deal. And with Tom doing enough work to cover the bases, it could be completely out in the open.

At the conclusion of their meal, John and Tom shook hands and agreed to discuss the idea further. Tom was interested in doing it, but he wanted to be sure he was covered. John was also interested in doing it, but he needed Tom to play along with him. Over the next month, the two would talk on the phone several times a day, working out the fine points of the conspiracy that would eventually lead to their mutual downfall.

CHAPTER FOUR
Good Soldier, Bad Orders

The next year – 2006 – began right where the previous year had left off, with John still battling with himself about the issue of Bermuda. He'd spent the entire Christmas holiday with the nagging thought in the back of his mind that there would come the time when he'd have to either put up or shut up, meaning he'd either have to approve the check or refuse to. His conscience told him it would do nothing but cause him more trouble than he could possibly imagine if he wrote the check. His better judgment told him that AIG was going to make his life a living hell if he didn't write it. He had found that emotional place that is so often referred to as being between a rock and a hard place.

In January, John sought out Axel Freudmann, who was at that time the Senior Vice President of Human Resources for all of AIG. Freudmann, John reasoned, would be in a position to advise him on how to proceed, given that he'd probably been in the same position at some point during his tenure at AIG. Freudmann, had he needed the money desperately enough, could have been a stand-in for Woody Allen. He was the son of a Jewish diamond merchant who came from the old way of thinking. Things like sexual harassment weren't part of his sphere of concern – he made jokes that he thought were funny, and if you were somehow offended by what he'd said, well, fuck you and the horse you rode in on. There was nothing politically correct about Axel. The opposite of Nottingham in every sense of the word, Freudmann was a complete and utter Francophile who made no apologies for it.

That said, if you happened to catch him on a bad day, it was best to steer clear as much as possible. He'd headed up the Human Resources department for twenty-eight years – he'd started under Hank Greenberg – and he did not take kindly to last-minute requests for days off or anything unplanned. It's not to say he wasn't fair; just that he liked to know about things long before they happened. And he valued his relationships with employees. He fostered them, nurtured them, did his best to keep lines of communication open. He often referred to AIG as a family. Because, like I said, he wanted to know what was going on before it happened. And he'd found over his years that the best way to ensure that he got that news was to get the gossip from the employees themselves, his family.

To that end, he had a regularly-scheduled meeting with everyone in HR, one-on-one, once a week. It was in that meeting – which was ostensibly for the purpose of updating him on projects employees were working on – that you dished out everything you knew in the hopes that he'd reward you later on when it was year-end performance review time. Because of the relationship he and Freudmann had developed, John felt comfortable enough telling him about his compunction in regards to the Bermuda entity, and specifically the payment that he'd been asked to make to Sevestre. In a way, that conversation began what was to become a very meaningful relationship between the two men.

John brought up the issue of Bermuda, and noticed an ever-so-slight change in Freudmann's facial expression. Had he been a trained poker player experienced in things like tells that give away a person's true thinking, John would have realized immediately that he'd struck a deep nerve with Axel. There was much hemming and hawing on Freudmann's part as he searched for the right words to explain the situation, and he finally settled on a deadpan, quiet tone that imparted a sense of conspiratorial agreement between the two men.

Axel went on to explain to John that he was aware that there had been some "problems" with the way the company had used the Bermuda payment entity in the past, some "issues" had arisen over specific methods of dispensing money via that payroll scheme. However, he followed-up, he wasn't "entirely sure" how those issues had been resolved. He made it a point not to say that the problems had, in fact, been cleared up; the only way that would have happened was if the scheme itself were no longer in use, which was clearly not the case. Instead, he opted for the safety of ambiguity and buck-passing. Sure he knew about AICO and sure he'd written a few checks off it himself. But he'd moved on. He'd done his tour of duty in the combat zone, and now he was enjoying his life as a civilian. Let somebody else get shot at for a while.

But he didn't completely abandon John without a life jacket. "Nothing in writing," he said to John at the end of the meeting. "You have any questions about Bermuda, you don't put it in writing. You don't email, you don't fax, you don't call. You have a question about Bermuda, you come talk to me face-to-face. Bermuda is a very touchy subject," he said. He stood, shook John's hand and thanked him for coming to see him. "Keep this thing under wraps," he added. "They've been using Bermuda since the days of Gene Famula," he said, referring to the man who had preceded Hoffman.

John understood all too well. He was, after all, a con artist himself, so he understood the need for secrecy in such instances. The more people that knew about a particular scam, the more chances there were for disaster. He was reminded of the advice given to American GIs writing home to loved ones during World War II about what they should and shouldn't say in their communications: "Loose lips sink ships." But John still had no idea how to proceed on the payment to Sevestre, so before he left the office, he pressed Freudmann for some advice that he could use to deal with the predicament. Freudmann advised him to go see Jacqueline Aguanno, the Head of Worldwide

Compensation for AIG. Aguanno worked directly for Freudmann, and it would turn out that she ran the Bermuda operation for the payroll department from her office in New York City.

By February of that year, John was feeling increased pressure from both Nottingham and Sevestre to write Sevestre his check. It struck both of them as odd that it was taking such a major effort on their collective parts to get the new kid in Human Resources to just do what he was told.

Armed with the information that he'd garnered from his meeting with Axel Freudmann, John requested a meeting with Nottingham. At that meeting – with Sevestre in attendance via telephone – John announced that, after his researching the matter to determine the best way to handle the situation within the parameters of the AIG corporate policies, the request would have to go through the AIG Compensation department, which meant that the request would have to go through Jacqueline Aguanno. He didn't mention the meeting with Freudmann; he didn't want to implicate Axel in this matter any more than he had to; he was a good soldier in that way. So he simply left it at Aguanno's having to approve the payment. And with that, the matter, Falcetta thought, would be final. He would be able to wash his hands of the whole thing, pass it off to Aguanno and leave it forever. He left the meeting and returned to his own office, thinking that things were all of a sudden looking up for him. He had a brief notion that perhaps he should call Pomboyno and put to rest their tentative deal, but the notion passed as quickly as it had appeared.

As a way of bolstering his own confidence in how to approach this situation, Falcetta met face-to-face with Jackie Aguanno following a staff meeting of the Human Resources Department. He explained to her the request – that he make a $50,000 payment via the Bermuda payroll to Marc Sevestre – and that he was uncomfortable with the idea of using what seemed to him to be a covert scheme that was used simply to funnel money and to help executives to avoid paying income taxes worldwide, especially in light of his discovery that it violated written AIG corporate policies.

Aguanno didn't flinch at the mention of the Bermuda program; she seemed neither surprised nor overly knowledgeable about the practice. Rather, she simply advised John that he should redirect the payment through the local French payroll department, which would be the office that normally handled Sevestre's compensation. It was, John noted to himself, just another toss in this game of hot-potato, where nobody wanted to hold the responsibility themselves for too long. It was outside the normal corporate compensation system, and nobody wanted to be the one left holding the pen when the payment was issued. And yet nobody wanted to step up and provide a definitive prohibition on the continued use of the Bermuda company either. Nobody, it seemed, except John Falcetta.

John once again went to see Nottingham, explaining to him that Aguanno had advised him that the payment should be made via French payroll rather than the Bermuda account. Nottingham, however, was insistent that John specifically not go through French payroll. John explained that he would be seeking further information about how best to proceed; it was at this meeting with Ken that John first mentioned the fact that he would be meeting weekly with Axel, and that he would include on his agenda for these weekly meetings the Bermuda practice and how best to help Nottingham manage the situation.

At the next meeting he had with Freudmann, John again broached the Bermuda practice. Freudmann valued loyalty as highly as any other trait in a colleague, and the fact that John had maintained a degree of secrecy in regards to Bermuda pleased him tremendously. Whether or not he thought John was engaged in a wild goose chase as he worked to get rid of the practice that had been in place for decades is immaterial. What is important is that he offered John advice on how best to proceed at this point, given Falcetta's continued misgivings about the whole practice. He advised John to engage an outside consultant, a neutral third-party of sorts, that could better examine the situation through objective lenses and decide how best to proceed.

John was initially surprised by the suggestion. Why, he wondered, shouldn't the issue be taken directly to PriceWaterhouseCoopers, the firm AIG kept on retainer for issues related to taxes and audit-related issues?

Freudmann didn't answer directly. Rather, he instructed John to contact Stanton Young, a corporate tax attorney, as well as Marc Bernstein from the AIG Corporate Counsel's office. He made it a point to tell John that he should not discuss this matter with Sullivan, Tse, Bernstein or anyone associated with PriceWaterhouseCoopers.

Stanton Young's was a name that seemed to come up with regularity any time Bermuda was mentioned, especially when the word "tax" was paired with it. He'd been at AIG thirty years and looked every bit the part of an AIG lifer. His clothes and hair were usually rather rumpled-looking, and he had half-moon glasses that hung around his neck, suspended by a lanyard. The effect was a picture of a man who was a slave to his job and who worked way too many hours, yet managed to barely get a dent in his to-do pile by day's end. And the reality is that he was overworked. He knew US tax laws inside and out, but foreign issues – like ones dealing with French payroll issued off of a Bermuda corporation – were alien subjects to him. But, as any truly intelligent person will do, Stanton admitted when he didn't know the answers. And though he knew the use of the Bermuda scheme wasn't within the normal corporate compensation system, he wasn't going to speak specifically to the issues with Sevestre, because that involved French tax law. In other words, outside his expertise so outside his sphere of problems that he needed to deal with.

Bernstein was a Harvard Law graduate, with a capital HAR and VARD. He dropped what people referred to as "the H-bomb" when he could get it into a conversation, and he had trouble hiding his bitterness at working for an HR guy at AIG – and if he'd only known how academically unqualified that particular HR guy was, he'd no doubt have been even more bitter.

That said, John recalled a time when Marc introduced him to his children. Marc introduced John, telling the kids that he was "Daddy's friend" as opposed to "Daddy's co-worker" or something similar. It was, to John's mind, a touching display to see a father separate his personal life and his work life, and to keep his children from having to enter the latter. It was a brief moment, but one that made a huge impression on John and definitely gave John a soft spot in his heart for Bernstein.

In March, Falcetta met with both Young and Bernstein, and they were joined by Karen Hansen from AIG's Internal Tax department. Karen was one of those women every boss wants to hire. She was a hard worker, quiet, pleasant to be around. And she had a sexy librarian look about her that drove men crazy. After listening to John explain the practice of using Bermuda for split-payroll activities and bonus payments – he more than once referenced the "open checkbook" comments so many of his colleagues had used – the trio told him that this was the first they'd heard of the practice.

Finally, John thought to himself, *I found somebody that isn't in on the scam*.

After some brief discussion, the group agreed with John's original view that this act was explicitly illegal, and could be a titanic problem for the corporate giant. That was, however, where the agreement ended. As the collected brains argued about how best to proceed, John's mind again returned to the hot-potato game that he'd been a part of with the Sevestre payment. But now, instead of nobody wanting to be left holding the pen, the game now was to see who would have to be the one to tell the beneficiaries of this scam that the game was up and they were up to their necks in boiling water, and the level was rising quickly. John would later remark, "It was actually a lot of fun watching all of them dance around like trained monkeys."

In the end, in what seemed to have become the status quo method of handling issues relating to Bermuda by now, the group as a whole decided yet again to collectively pass the buck. Everyone looked to Young to be the authority on this, and when Stanton said he thought that somebody outside the firm – somebody that they could control – was the best option, everyone fell in lock-step behind him and agreed. An "outside consultant" – wink, wink – was decided on as the best course of action. Falcetta was instructed to locate said "outside consultant;" it was assumed by all present that he knew what they meant and that he would know of someone who could clear up this mess with no fanfare and no publicity. In other words, John was to find somebody who could find a way out of this boondoggle, and keep it quiet all at the same time. After all, Edmund Tse's name was on the list, and the whole thing had somehow become John's problem to solve.

Falcetta got the hint, and contacted a former co-worker of his from his days at Lehman Brothers, a lawyer named Charles Oswald. Oswald runs a firm called CEO Law, whose website boasts that the firm "offers a nuanced blend of practice areas designed to engage and address a unique set of key legal and business issues *before* their unexpected discovery during compliance, IPO, financing, private sale or other critical due diligence investigations" (emphasis theirs). To John's mind, that was a nice way of saying, "We fix your biggest fuck-ups before the feds get wise and throw you in prison." It was the perfect firm to advise AIG on the matter of Bermuda.

"Black-bag operations" were strategies employed by the Federal Bureau of Investigation and, no doubt, other more clandestine groups, until the Supreme Court declared the practice unconstitutional in 1972. Before that monumental decision, however, specialists would regularly employ such techniques as lock-picking, wire-tapping, forgery and whatever other skills would allow them to better act in total secrecy as they worked to accomplish their goals. Black-bag operations are often relegated to the likes of James Bond films and spy novels about the Cold War. But 007 is a movie character and the Cold War ended long ago. This was the twenty-first century, and black-bag operations had been outlawed nearly forty years prior.

Legal issues and historical tid-bits aside, this was quickly becoming a black-bag operation.

$$* \qquad * \qquad *$$

While the accounting and legal folks were dancing and everyone involved in the Bermuda mess was tossing the hot-potato, John was still developing his own deal on the sidelines. He and Pomboyno by now had spoken many times as they fine-tuned their plan to set up a dummy corporate head-hunting firm. The two agreed to meet for lunch at Smith & Wollensky steak-house on 49th Street, a restaurant populated mostly by executives from Midtown and the Upper East Side. It was a perfect place for the pair to meet, as two guys in custom-made suits talking business over lunch wouldn't even register as a blip on anybody's radar should anybody be looking for blips. And given his history, John knew how easily blips could show up when you least expected them.

John brought with him to that meeting several documents. He brought copies of a few open position listings that AIG was looking to fill. Nothing extraordinary, but positions that were high enough up on the food chain to require the efforts of an outside search firm to fill. Tom had decided that his new "business" would be named Enterprise Search Associates. When Tom submitted invoices for his "services" to AIG's HR Department, John would approve and pay them. He reminded Tom that he would need to keep the invoice amounts under $50,000. Over that threshold, and Falcetta would need additional approval to pay; less than fifty grand, and John could approve payments until the cows came home without anybody else saying a word about it. Had he been so inclined, John would have suggested to his superiors at AIG that this sort of single-line signage authority – which was prevalent across many departments within AIG's corporate holdings – has no control mechanism and allows for people to take advantage of the system in a variety of ways. He was not so inclined, however, so he kept quiet about it.

As the two pored over the documents, John advised Tom to proceed with setting up the dummy company. Because Tom was going to be providing real leads with real résumés – and because he was a real insurance salesman who could speak the language – the risk of getting caught was low. But just to be on the extra safe side of things, John suggested that they bring in two other AIG colleagues – he didn't want to bring them in on the scam, but rather just to their meetings, so as to keep the relationship out in the open, lest any prying eyes get suspicious – and so Falcetta invited Paul Rix and Dennis Zampella to join them at their next meeting.

Rix was the embodiment of an English gentleman. From his understated Rolex watch that told the world he appreciated fine craftsmanship but didn't want to flaunt his income level to the fact that, despite handling IT projects that were in the 100- to 200-million-dollar range, he always made time for anybody that needed his help on a project, Paul was a corporate dream. He would always stand up for those working under him when they needed his support, and he had the respect of everyone around him. He once told John that he'd noticed "real improvement in the people products for the first time in years" since John's arrival at AIG.

Zampella was a former director for US operations of BMW who had moved to AIG a few years before John. He was a friendly guy with a quick wit and the occasional bit of Italian folk wisdom to offer. He had a ton of money and was always willing to go to lunch with a colleague, but he never seemed to be able to find his wallet when the bill arrived at the table. This pair of men would become John's cover; both were involved, to some extent, with recruitment of AIG executives, so both could vouch for the fact that John's dealings with Pomboyno were legitimate. Legitimate in the sense that they were at least talking about business over lunch and seeing candidates that Pomboyno had identified.

AIG had two types of business relationships with headhunting groups, retainer and contingency. Retainer agreements were the same sort of agreement someone has with an attorney or accountant or similar professional. Namely, you pay a set amount up-front (the retainer), and the professional acting on your behalf deducts his pay from the retainer as he goes forward. In AIG's case, retainers were paid in three installments: the first third was paid when the agency signed a contract with AIG; the second installment was paid 30 to 45 days following the original payment, pending what was loosely defined as "satisfactory progress" on the part of the search group, progress that was proven by a written report submitted by the headhunter; the third installment was paid when a candidate identified by the search group was successfully placed with AIG. Contingency agreements, on the other hand were more of a commission-style of arrangement. The headhunter on contingency would be paid in full when a successful search resulted in AIG's hiring the candidate identified by the headhunter, and not before.

Regardless of the payment arrangement, headhunters had to be on an approved list of vendors – a list that John Falcetta not only had access to, but one to which he had the power to add vendors at his own discretion – and they had to have a signed contract with AIG to participate in the search process as required. Both of these formalities were pretty easy to take care of. John simply had his secretary add Enterprise Search Associates as an approved vendor of services and issued them a contract to engage in the search for appropriate candidates to fill empty positions as required by AIG. The contract was contingency-based, so when ESA successfully located and placed a candidate within a position at AIG, Pombonyo would get paid for his services.

Before their next meeting, Tom set up Enterprise Search Associates, and got his federal tax ID number. He had also opened a corporate checking account and used his business office in Melville, New York, on Long Island. He got phone and fax numbers, an answering service, everything he'd need in order to pass as a legitimate business. The pair – this time joined by Rix and Zampella – met for lunch again, this time at Captain's Ketch, inside the Tower at 70 Pine Street. John put lunch on his expense account – it was, after all, a business-related lunch with a headhunter, as Rix and Zampella could attest – and John and Tom discussed some current positions that needed filling at AIG. Tom agreed to set to work immediately, and when the group members parted that afternoon, the game was afoot.

John returned to his office in the Tower and Tom to his in Long Island. John sent over copies of bills that had been submitted by legitimate headhunters that AIG had recently paid. The idea was for Tom to have a template from which to work when submitting his own bills. The closer he could come to actual bills, the less likely the chance there would be any issues with payment.

Within a few weeks, Tom had done minimal amounts of work, but had still managed to produce a few impressive résumés through some advertisements he'd run in various publications and online, résumés that were impressive enough to get the attention of Zampella and Rix. Pomboyno submitted invoices for his services but, as he was on contingency, he wouldn't get paid until the candidates were actually hired by AIG. So the pair sat and waited and hoped. But the résumés went nowhere.

Soon after, Pomboyno's phone rang. It was an outside verification service, a service that was about as thorough as the one who'd performed John's own background check, the one that had somehow believed his story about mistaken identity. This call to Pomboyno was simply to verify his existence as a headhunter. Because his answering service answered all calls by saying, "Thank you for calling Enterprise Search Associates. How may I direct your call?" it was game-set-match as far as the verification service was concerned. They'd called the number they'd been given, the secretary had answered with the appropriate greeting, it was legitimate. They asked to speak to Pomboyno, and their call was transferred to him. Tom verified the information they were looking into – yes, he was Tom Pomboyno, yes he was the principal in Enterprise Search Associates (no need to mention that he was the only associate), yes the tax identification number they had on file was accurate. And that was it. The only hurdle he needed to clear had been cleared. He was now eligible to receive payments from Falcetta for services performed.

At that point, John decided to take a risky step. He submitted the invoices Tom had previously sent – the ones paired with the résumés that had not resulted in candidates' getting hired – and approved checks to pay those bills. This was problematic, given that Tom was on contingency and not retainer. In other words, until he successfully placed a candidate, there should have been no payment made to him. But the checks were issued and no eyebrows were raised. About a week later, Tom and John met for lunch once more at Smith & Wollensky, this time alone. At that lunch, Tom presented John with a check made out to "HCMP," an acronym which stood for Human Capital Management Partners.

Human Capital Management Partners – as ambiguous and misleading a name that was ever attached to a business – was drawn from a term that entered the American business lexicon in the early twenty-first century, no doubt playing on the elaborate titles ascribed to low-ranking employees with increasing frequency. Basically Human Resources gurus decided that the guys in finance weren't the only ones dealing with capital. They felt that their own contributions – namely the management of those in the workforce – qualified as capital management, too, and thus the term "human capital management" was born. So what better name to ascribe to a holding company that was little more than a bank account owned by a Human Resources executive who didn't want his name – John Falcetta – on it, so that he could better hide things from those who might be looking for them? That check was the first of many kickbacks that John would receive from his friend.

It was, he freely admits, a greedy act on his part. He wanted to live the good life. He wanted to provide a better life for his family. He wanted to get his share of AIG's money. He was, after all, being asked to conspire to continue a massive fraud, yet he wasn't benefitting from that conspiracy himself, so he felt he deserved this. And he felt, too, that he was being passively threatened with the loss of his job. Whatever rationale he decided on, it didn't matter in the end. It all boiled down to greed, plain and simple. He admits today that if he had it all to do over again, he wouldn't have engaged in it, but then again, hindsight is a luxury that few of us have the ability to actually act on. At the time, it seemed easy, just like all those scams from his earlier days. Too easy, probably. And what's more, in John's mind, even if it was stealing, it was stealing from AIG, the company that from his view was participating in a scheme to avoid disclosure of payments to its employees, more often than not in apparent contradiction with its legal obligations in a variety of countries. John saw himself as something of a corporate Robin Hood, in that regard, stealing from the richest to line the pockets of the less rich.

But once he accepted that check, he'd gone through yet one more of the many doors he'd already walked through in his lifetime, doors that only allowed you to go one direction. And once you went through them, you couldn't turn around and go back out. As Willie Wonka told his confused factory guests, "You've gotta' go forwards to go back. Better press on." John took those words to heart. He pressed on. He continued to work the scam as best he could. He really had no choice at this point; there was no going back now.

CHAPTER FIVE
"We Stopped Doing That Years Ago"

The black-bag operation designed to clean up the mess created by the Bermuda situation was in full effect by May of 2006. Charles Oswald met with Falcetta in New York, and John briefed him on the situation. Oswald was a tall man, a devout Christian with a beard, glasses and a deep voice. He always struck John as the perfect minister. He always dressed meticulously, as was proper for a man of his status as international man of mystery. He was a bit of an eccentric, too – it was his habit (or perhaps compulsion) to have a single scoop of vanilla ice cream every night before bed and he had a personal answering service that shut off his home phone from ringing at nine o'clock every night on the dot. Eccentricities aside, if you were running a war room, Oswald was the man you wanted at your right hand.

At that first meeting, John made sure to emphasize that this must not be traceable back to AIG, which played right into Oswald's specialization. The orders for absolute secrecy had come down from Freudmann himself, with instructions for John to test the waters, so to speak, by giving Oswald just the information on Greece, the United Kingdom and France, three of the countries where executives were facing the possibility of legal issues arising from their use of the Bermuda payment program.

Oswald spent a month researching the situation and looking into the legal implications and options that were available to AIG. John turned over to him every document he'd been given – the only copies of those documents – by Dozier and Rhotla eight months earlier. He and Oswald communicated, initially, via email. And even though their emails had subject lines of "ALICO

Payroll Project" and cryptic content that made no specific mention to the Bermuda payment practice, the word came down again from Axel Freudmann that there was to be nothing in writing, electronic or otherwise, in regards to Bermuda. Honoring that request, Oswald called John to relay to him his preliminary thoughts on the matter in person.

John took notes at that meeting – lots of notes – and as he perused them afterwards, what he'd suspected was going to be true came to be. Oswald's findings weren't good news for AIG. Basically his message was that AIG had dug itself into a pretty deep hole, and there was little he could do to change what they'd done. The thing about money is that there's always a paper trail, no matter how much you try to launder or soak or bleach. You can't get rid of it altogether, especially when you were talking about the amounts of money these guys were throwing around. Over the years, hundreds of AIG executives worldwide had benefitted from the program. Oswald and Falcetta together estimated that, over time, the amount of money could have easily exceeded $500 million, not including stock and option payments. The implications were more than a couple of spreadsheets could handle.

After hearing Oswald's take on the situation as it pertained to France – and, more specifically, as it pertained to John's making a payment to Sevestre via Bermuda – John made his final decision in regards to the check he'd been asked to issue so many months ago. He was putting his foot down; he was refusing to write it. He phoned Dawn Cherouyze, who headed up the HR office for ALICO SA (the French division of ALICO) and instructed her to make the requested payment to Sevestre via the French payroll office as if it were a normal compensation payment.

At first, Dawn sounded somewhat confused by the request. She seemed to think that there was no reason Sevestre wouldn't be paid via the French office, and wondered why John felt compelled to call and instruct her to do so.

He gave her a brief explanation about what had been going on with his hesitation to write a check off the Bermuda account. She cut him off before he could get too into it, though, and told him that the French office had stopped doing Bermuda payments long ago, as they'd determined it was "illegal in France" to do so. And while it wasn't a newsflash to John that income tax evasion via offshore accounts was against French law, the fact that they'd supposedly stopped the procedure shocked him.

The biggest bombshell of the conversation, however, was that Dawn repeated how odd she thought it was that he'd be calling, because she recalled specifically being asked to stop doing all such payments for those people in France who had reported directly to "Mr. Sullivan," as she had called him, when Mr. Sullivan had had people in that part of the world reporting directly to him.

The "Mr. Sullivan" she was referring to was none other than the Chief Executive Officer of AIG, Mr. Martin Sullivan himself. One of the men Axel had specifically advised John against talking to about the program.

John hung up the phone and began to wonder how much deception was required to keep this scheme going, not to mention who had known what when.

He brought Oswald back to New York at the end of June, and trotted him out like an expert witness at a trial. First to Marc Bernstein then on to Karen Hansen and finally to Stanton Young. All three agreed – in their separate meetings – that it had been an excellent idea to bring in an outside party to assess the issue. And while none of them verbalized it, John knew it was because none of them wanted to risk being the one that got caught with their hands in the cookie jar when Mom got home.

At John's suggestion, they all three agreed – again, in separate meetings – that it would be best for Oswald to continue his work, and that he be allowed greater access to the files pertaining to Bermuda so that he might assess the liabilities from the global perspective. From there, they could figure out how big the problem was really going to be overall. John knew, though, that even the initial estimates were big enough to sink the Bismarck.

The strategy worked out brilliantly for all involved. Oswald got to continue billing by the hour in fifteen-minute increments and AIG could honestly say, if anybody came snooping around, that they were "looking into" the issue and would be able to comment more fully when they had a better understanding of the scope of the problem. Luckily for them, nobody came knocking.

In July, no doubt as a response to John's conversation with Dawn Cherouyze regarding Bermuda, John received an anonymous document from the French office. It was a report produced by FIDAL Direction Internationale, an international tax law firm located in the La Défense section of western Paris. The report, authored by Didier Hoff, was dated March 20, 2006, was addressed to Ludwig Baruchel, the Chief Operating Officer of AIG Vie, the French branch of AIG. The report didn't pull any punches; it laid out the facts in the first paragraph:

"We understand that, until January 1, 2006, part of the variable compensation of some AIG Vie executives was paid through an entity located in Bermuda. This variable compensation paid through Bermuda was not recharged to any entity located in France or abroad and, thus, was not subject to any French or foreign Social Security taxes. In addition, said amounts were not subject to any withholding income tax (in France or abroad) and we also understand that the beneficiaries of that offshore compensation did not, in France, self-report such income to the tax authorities on their annual tax returns. In other words, said amounts paid through Bermuda were not subject to any taxes anywhere and, thus, 100% of said amounts went directly into the beneficiaries' pockets."

What John found most interesting about this communication was the fact that the law firm's report included hard data, specifically numbers related to amounts owed by AIG Vie and the individuals who had benefitted from the split payroll activities. In terms of the Social Security taxes due, Hoff wrote, "Based on the annual compensation of the executives involved, we can estimate the Social Security taxes past due at around 65% of gross variable compensation undisclosed for 2003, 2004 and 2005." The news for the individuals involved wasn't any better: "Therefore, we can estimate the past income tax that the beneficiaries owe at around 55% of the unreported variable compensation."

There were three individual executives named in the report as being the men involved in the scheme, at least insofar as this particular report was concerned: Ludwig Baruchel, Chief Operating Officer of ALICO SA and a member of ALICO SA's Board of Directors; Joël Farre, Chief Executive Officer of ALICO SA; and Marc Sevestre, President of the Board of ALICO SA and President of ALICO SA, not to mention the indirect cause of all the recent flap in the New York City headquarters.

The issue of how to make things right with the authorities was the real meat of the letter. The obvious solution — just stop doing it and pretend it never happened — wasn't a viable option if the executives named in the report planned on keeping their current pay levels:

"The disclosure of all variable compensation as of January 1, 2006, would, indeed, increase the risk of audits by either the Social Security (AIG Vie's risk) or the tax administration (executives' risk) since the 'jump' in compensation could not be explained. Therefore, it would be wise to increase the three executives' compensation by compensation items paid by another group entity or an equity mechanism, and not AIG Vie.

"Regarding the payment of the variable compensation by another group entity, we suggest either the implementation of UK directors' fees or US employment contracts.

"Regarding the use of an equity mechanism, the increase in compensation can be replaced by either a grant of qualified options over the AIG US stocks or by a grant of qualified RSUs over AIG US stocks. The latter mechanism, where RSUs are granted by the parent company in the US, would be the best solution since the number of RSUs to be granted could easily be calculated by referring to the Fair Market Value of the RSUs under FAS 123 R and would, under a French Qualified Plan, avoid the payment of Social Security taxes, thereby reducing the executives' employments costs."

What that all meant was that the FIDAL legal minds were suggesting that it would be impossible to just resume full payment off the local payroll, due to the fact that the tax authorities would see a major jump in reported income, which would likely trigger an audit and blow the lid off the whole thing. So instead, they were suggesting that AIG consider offering Restricted Stock Units (RSUs) – restricted shares of AIG's US stock – as compensation instead of actual cash. It was the easiest way to hide what would be a spike in the executives' pay, because the shares didn't have to be reported as income until they were sold. So on paper, they would have been making the same amount of taxable income annually as they had been during the Bermuda payment years. In terms of their tax obligation, they'd be making the same amount as they had been under the Bermuda plan; in reality, they'd be making the same amount as they had been under the Bermuda plan, too, with the exception that the remainder would be a deferred compensation in the form of restricted stock shares.

With all of the damaging information contained in the report, it didn't surprise John too much to see hand-written notes all over it: "Should be deleted from our PC and from the PC of FIDAL" was scribbled across the top of the first page. Good advice, to be sure.

After he'd read through the report's thirteen pages a few times, John grew increasingly disgusted in what was going on. He began to make phone calls to various AIG offices around the world, calls to his fellow HR colleagues who were in the same position as he was in different divisions. His first call was to Mike Festo, a Senior Vice President in AIG Human Resources who had worked for Martin Sullivan. Festo said unequivocally that the practice of split-payroll via Bermuda had been terminated years earlier under direct orders from Hank Greenberg.

John's next call was to Connie Miller, the Head of Global Human Resources of AIG Investments. She echoed Mike's contention that the practice had been stopped several years prior due to legal issues.

He got the same answers from both Lynda Wood, Director of Human Resources in AIG's United Kingdom headquarters, and Dawn Cherouyze in Paris. All four of them told John that without any shred of doubt, the practice had been stopped altogether, no exceptions.

And what's more, each of the four HR executives he spoke with were equally unequivocal about the fact that both Aguanno and Freudmann were well aware of the fact that the order had come down that the practice was to stop immediately several years prior. The order had come down after none other than the Internal Revenue Service had ordered a stop to the practice. Aguanno, in fact, had been put in charge of terminating the practice along with help from Freudmann in 2001.

John immediately went back to his mentor, Tom Hoffman, to figure out what exactly he should believe about the situation. He laid it out for Hoffman, telling him everything about the phone conversations he'd had recently with his colleagues and the FIDAL report. Hoffman also told John that Aguanno and Freudmann were well aware of the fact that the practice was supposed to have been terminated across all divisions. But they'd knowingly allowed it to continue in the Life Insurance division because, as Tom put it, "Edmund Tse wanted it that way."

Now that he fully understood what he was working against, John felt that he had done all that he could with the Bermuda situation. In his mind, the fraud had gotten too big and too out of hand for him to handle, and he figured it had also gotten too big for Oswald to just sweep it away with a few presses of the right buttons on a computer keyboard.

And the more research Oswald did, the more Oswald himself came to that same conclusion. He reported his findings to John in periodic phone calls — again, there was to be nothing in writing — and John finally went to see Freudmann about the depth and scope of the whole situation. And though he didn't let Freudmann know about his conversation with Tom Hoffman, John did give him the information that he'd gotten from Oswald, all of which was damaging enough on its own. Freudmann instructed John to get Jackie Aguanno involved immediately. Of all the names Freudmann could have pulled out for John to bring in, Jackie's was the one that didn't surprise him in the slightest.

That instruction from Freudmann was music to John's ears. His feelings were that Jackie had been involved in the conspiracy to cover it up from the start — as had Freudmann — and if anybody deserved to go down with the ship, he'd be happy to vote for her. John met with her and told her the same thing he'd told Freudmann, namely that based on the information Oswald had provided him, he felt that he was completely out of his league and that something major would need to be done. Jackie requested a meeting with Oswald so that she could discuss it directly with him, and John set up that meeting.

Several months after his first meeting with John Falcetta in May of that

year, Oswald met with Aguanno in John's office. At that time, Oswald outlined what he felt were the options – which were basically to either fall on their
collective sword or hide and hope, because there weren't enough black bags in
the world to fix this one – and Aguanno looked increasingly ill the longer she
listened. When he was done, Aguanno was silent for a moment. Finally she
said bluntly, "You should know that this thing goes all the way to the top. It's
way over my head."

The subtext of that statement, at least to John's mind, was that she was
trying to absolve herself. After all, if people above her knew what was happening, then she could argue that she was just a soldier taking orders. The finger-
pointing was beginning in earnest now that the reality was setting in. The rats
were abandoning the sinking ship. John already knew that Senior Vice
Chairman Edmund Tse was benefitting from the conspiracy, and that the CEO
of AIG had at least been tangentially involved in that, even if he hadn't been
accepting payments via Bermuda, he was aware of the practice's existence. And
that meant that Sullivan was just as guilty as anybody who'd accepted money
directly.

John threw his hands up in the air – literally – and announced to the
others that he was officially withdrawing from the operation, because it had
gotten too big for him. He then asked Oswald to transition the control of the
investigation from himself to Jackie Aguanno. Before relinquishing control in
full, however, John asked Jackie point-blank why the practice hadn't been terminated for ALICO when it was terminated in all other divisions that had been
involved with it.

She told him flatly, "All the divisions did stop it way back when, and
then we started it back up for the international executives." That was the
extent of her explanation to John, who let it go, as he was more interested in
just getting it off his plate on to hers as soon as possible.

Over the course of the meeting, John found himself talking less and listening more, as Aguanno and Oswald talked about the situation. At times, they spoke as if John weren't in the room. He sat and listened, and the longer he did so, the more clear it became that Jackie had been complicit in this scheme for years, working together with Hoffman and Freudmann to keep it going for ALICO. It occurred to John at some point during the discussion that his concerns about the program had been handed back-and-forth between Aguanno and Hoffman intentionally, no doubt as they stalled to try and figure out how to handle it. He grew increasingly resentful towards everyone involved. It was then that he had the first real fear that they would try to move him out the door and that he would need to start documenting what he was seeing, so that he could have his own trump card to play if the need for that sort of leverage ever arose. Aguanno and Oswald, in their defense, could reason this was "business as usual," not recognizing the impropriety.

From that point forward, Oswald worked directly with Aguanno. He checked in with John periodically, at John's request, to give him updates on what he was finding out. John assumed that Jackie wouldn't have allowed Oswald to communicate with him, but given that they'd been co-workers so long ago, Oswald still felt a kinship with John that went beyond standard workplace arrangements. Oswald told him of the seriousness of the offenses he'd been uncovering. It was, he told John, a massive worldwide scheme that had benefitted hundreds and hundreds of AIG executives. He also said he'd been working with Alice Harrison, the Manager of Corporate Compensation for AIG, who had confirmed the scope of the scheme over the years.

Following-up on one of Oswald's early recommendations, Jackie Aguanno informed Edmund Tse about the investigation, though she didn't let him know everything Oswald had told her about the potential severity of the trouble. Perhaps she assumed that, at this point, it was best to just keep him informed on a need-to-know basis, and she didn't think he needed to know everything just yet. Tse showed John several memos that an anonymous lawyer had been coaxed into writing at some point in the 80's. These memos offered the legal opinion that the Bermuda practice was legal. He then asked John to draft similar ones, memos professing the same opinion as to the legality of the practice, and specifically telling John what dates to put on them, dates that were not anywhere near accurate.

The purpose of this whole process of back-dating memos was so that, if the need arose, Tse could point to those memos and claim total, blissful ignorance, because he was just doing what he'd been told was legal. So it wouldn't be his fault. It would be somebody else's fault. John had a bad feeling the "somebody else" was going to be him when push came to shove, because it would be his name that any investigator would find on the back-dated memo saying it was legal. John eventually agreed to write them after Edmund implied his job depended on his writing them: "If you don't write them," he asked John, "what do I need you here for?"

In the end, Oswald presented Jackie Aguanno with a formal report of his findings, which was a report that ran about two-hundred-and-fifty pages. In it, he outlined the fact that AIG had willfully violated tax laws in twenty to thirty countries, and would be responsible for payment of millions upon millions of dollars in back taxes, not to mention penalties and interest. And there would certainly be an investigation into how they'd managed to evade paying so much tax for so long. From there, it wouldn't be a long time before fingers began pointing at individual employees of AIG, namely those that had benefitted over the years from the Bermuda scheme. Oswald had just lobbed a grenade into Jackie's office.

The greatest concern for AIG wasn't the money. It was, rather, the risk of severe global sanction. AIG had plenty of money to pay the back taxes – they could have easily paid all the taxes, plus interest and penalties, for all of the employees who had benefitted from the Bermuda payment scheme – but that wasn't the issue. As a US-based corporation operating in places like France, Greece, Hong Kong, the United Kingdom and any of the other foreign countries in which AIG had offices, they operated with a foreign business license. If the regulatory and financial ministries of those countries got a whiff of the fact that AIG was conspiring to defraud them of income tax revenues, then AIG could have its license to operate in those countries revoked. And that would have started an avalanche of financial disaster within the Tower.

Had Jackie Aguanno been following standard procedure – that is, if there can be said to be a standard procedure to follow when working on a massive cover-up – she would have taken the report to Axel Freudmann to discuss it. From there, Freudmann probably would have gone to Falcetta who, despite his distaste for the whole practice, would have worked to affect as slow a burn on the whole thing as he could, thereby lessening the damage. But Jackie didn't follow standard procedure. She went straight to the head of AIG's legal team, Anastasia Kelly, AIG's General Counsel who reported directly to Sullivan and Tse.

On or about December 15, 2006, Kelly was fully informed about what was going on. At that point, she immediately ordered a "hard stop" on all payments from Bermuda. In investing circles, a hard stop is an order put in place by an investor that dictates that when a security reaches a certain price, an automatic sell order is sent out. In the case of illegal payments issued by AIG, it meant don't do it anymore, no matter who tells you to for what purpose. No checks written off Bermuda, plain and simple. Tse's back-dated memos would now be a moot point; if there were no payments being authorized, there was no need for him to produce memos explaining why he wasn't to blame for getting his payments via Bermuda. Edmund Tse immediately got on the phone to John Falcetta. John's description of the call was simple and to the point: "It got ugly."

Word of the hard stop on Bermuda payments spread quickly through the office, not to mention through the world. Within twenty-four hours, John had been summoned to Martin Sullivan's office to discuss what exactly was going on. At that meeting, Sullivan told Falcetta, "We stopped doing that years ago." It went without saying what "that" Sullivan was referring to. "Why in the world did Tse and Freudmann keep it going after we put a stop to it?"

John had no answer to give him. He'd just been following orders, but he wasn't about to pull that card right now. It hadn't worked very well at Nuremberg, and he was pretty sure it wasn't going to work a whole lot better at that exact moment. So he shook his head and said he would continue to work on the matter with both Jackie Aguanno and Anastasia Kelly. But the part of his brain that loved doing the *New York Times* crossword had begun connecting the dots. After his conversation with Dawn Cherouyze, he'd started figuring a few things out.

It wasn't a coincidence that Sullivan had gotten all of the people who reported to him directly removed from the Bermuda payroll. John guessed that Sullivan had put a stop to the process in his division in 2005; it was possible, John mused, that he'd given up a few years earlier, in 2002, when he'd been appointed to AIG's Board of Directors. It wouldn't be necessarily proper for a member of the Board to be receiving illegal tax-free payments; it certainly wouldn't be proper for the CEO of AIG to be receiving them. But by now, nothing surprised John, and he wasn't entirely sure which way was up and who was up to what.

The timing was immaterial at this point, though. What mattered to John was that Sullivan knew about the practice – had been directly involved with it, in fact – and was probably aware of the fact that it was continuing today, despite his feigned ignorance to the existence of the whole thing. Within days, Rod Martin was named Chairman of the Bermuda operations. He was replacing Edmund Tse.

As the week wore on, several protesting voices grew louder, crying foul that they'd lost their tax-free payments. Among the most vocal were some names that were relatively high up on the corporate chain of command, including Edmund Tse, Senior Vice Chairman of AIG's Life Insurance Division; Andreas Vassiliou, ALICO Senior Vice President and Regional CEO of ALICO Operations in Central and Eastern Europe; Patrick Choffell, Regional President of ALICO for the Middle East, Africa and South Asia; and Ricardo Garcia, President of ALICO for Latin America. All of them were deeply involved with the Bermuda payment program as recipients of tax-free payments from the covert account. All of these recipients had one major thing in common: They were all friends with Nottingham, with whom so much of this all started.

Edmund Tse, who was among the most vocal of the vocal, called John into his office. At that meeting, Tse demanded an explanation for what had happened and why it was that he would no longer be benefitting from a split-payroll arrangement. Just as he had with Sullivan, John served up Aguanno and Freudman as the sacrificial lambs; he couldn't hold back any longer. But he felt a little more on-level with Tse, so he threw in the detail that he'd been working with Oswald and Freudmann, who'd sent him to Aguanno, who in turn was the one that had gone straight to Anastasia Kelly. He hadn't intended for the conversation to be a ratting-out of Freudmann; rather, he was just trying to deflect the blame from himself, as he thought there was plenty to go around.

As it turned out, John had unintentionally been a rat. Freudmann was fired soon after. The actual firing took place ten days after Edmund Tse had stopped receiving his payments via Bermuda. It was also two days before huge bonus payments were to be made to the entire list of those who received money via the Bermuda scheme, payments which would now be coming through more traditional – and reportable – avenues.

*   *   *

While grenades were landing in executives' offices in the AIG Tower, John and Tom Pomboyno continued to work their headhunting scam. The first invoices that John had paid had made it through whatever due diligence the auditing department might have done – which was apparently none too exacting – and that success, as had happened in his past scams, bred confidence. And that confidence led him to greater risks. And he was inclined to take those risks, due to the fact that the global tax evasion scheme had hit the proverbial fan, which meant that John was now "expendable." He knew his days at AIG were numbered.

In June of 2006, Tom and John met at Il Vagabondo, a famous Italian restaurant on New York's Upper East Side known for having arguably the best veal parmegiana in the city. It also has the distinction of having its own indoor bocce court. It was an appropriate choice on so many levels, given that the restaurant's name translates to "the vagabond," a word that means, among other things, "a rogue." At that meeting, John received yet another envelope with a check made out to HCMP.

By July, the conspirators were growing increasingly confident. To this point, everything had gone smoothly with the invoices being submitted and checks being issued. No red flags had been raised, nothing had been said to John about the checks that were being issued to Pomboyno. John and Tom decided to meet at the Palm for their next meeting, at which AIG picked up the tab for prime rib and a bottle of outstanding Shafer Hills Select Cabernet. John put it on his corporate VISA, which would help prove the legitimacy of the relationship if anyone were to ask. With the heat increasing at the office, John suggested they up the stakes in this game they were playing. More invoices meant more money, so John suggested that Tom crank out several invoices and submit them for payment in the upcoming month.

A few weeks later, a fatter envelope arrived on John's desk, this one stuffed full of invoices from Tom. Everything moved through the system flawlessly until one of the HR staff members asked John who they should charge the fees back to, because their budget #654 didn't cover them. In other words, the main HR account – # 032-000-654 – hadn't been budgeted to cover these extra payments.

John's heart dropped through the floor as he thought he was caught for sure. Going over the budgeted amount would definitely cause some people to take notice, regardless of whether or not invoices were there to support the expenses. But then he remembered the slush fund – what they called "bench money" in the HR offices – that was a surplus account with about $4 million in it. The account was earmarked for any "special" projects that the HR execs might feel they needed a little extra money for. To John's mind, this little pet project of his fit that bill. That was the account that came to be the source of funding for all of the bogus invoices that would be submitted over the next several months.

John and Tom met at John's office in the AIG Tower to discuss further strategy. They were becoming increasingly brazen by now, as they thought they'd made it past the gates and were home free going forward. That month, they had their usual meeting – complete with the kickback exchange – inside the Senior Executive Dining Room right inside the Tower itself, where only the elite of AIG were entitled to eat. Access was limited through a special elevator code that one had to enter in order to get to the floor; after all, it just wouldn't do to be mixing with the riff-raff making less than a half-a-million a year. The irony of the fact that the men were carrying on the activities they were in the same dining room where Edmund Tse ate his lunch every day was not lost on either of the conspirators.

This pattern of lunching in very public places in order to do the money exchange became the common thread for John and Tom. They'd alternate between some of New York City's finest dining establishments, going to the Palm one month and Smith & Wollensky the following. One of John's personal favorites was a new place called Quality Meats, which features custom-cut steaks sold only at that particular restaurant and a steak sauce made tableside that John referred to as "awesome." The conspirators were eating and drinking like kings, all the while funneling off funds from AIG's coffers. This was, they both agreed, the easiest money they'd ever made in their lives. Not to mention some of the best free food.

The money was good. Very good, in fact. But John got greedy. He wanted more of this easy money. But there was more to it than that. John was aware on some level — just like all con men, both the good ones and the bad ones, are aware on some level — that this scheme couldn't last forever. The way he looked at things, he'd have two possible exit strategies, one good and one not-so-good. If he timed it right, he'd stop the scam at just the right moment before they all got caught. That would allow him to maximize his profits while minimizing his pain. He figured Edmund had it in for him by now, so there was nothing to lose.

In that sense, running a good scam is like buying a stock, which might explain why John was such a good cold caller for Merrill Lynch. When you buy a stock, the idea is to buy it at its lowest point and sell it at its highest point. Think of it this way: If you buy a stock at five dollars a share and sell it at twenty, you pocket fifteen dollars a share. If your buddy across the way buys that same stock on the same day as you at the same five dollars a share but holds on to it a day longer and sells it at twenty-one, he's making sixteen dollars a share. Of course, if he holds on to it for just one more day and it drops five dollars, he's kicking himself for not selling it the day before.

A good scam works the same way. If you get out at just the right moment, you look like a genius. But if you hold on just one day too long, you end up getting caught. And for John, getting caught would almost surely mean prison time. Unless, he reminded himself, he could broker a deal by leveraging the information he had on the Bermuda program. That, he hoped, would keep him out of jail. Bermuda was going to be his ace-in-the-hole.

Buoyed by his own growing self-confidence paired with his insatiable desire to make more money — and shielded, at least in part, by the knowledge that he had information that could potentially save him — John sought to expand the program by bringing in two additional colleagues who could contribute their own kickbacks to him after he got them set up in the system. The three headhunters would not know of each other's existence; John was the ringleader, and he felt that they didn't need to know each other. All that mattered was that they'd all be doing the same thing, namely submitting bogus invoices for work they hadn't performed and, in exchange for John's issuing them a check, they'd bounce some of that money back to John as a sort of thank-you gift. And three people giving him those thank-you gifts was three times as nice as one.

In September of 2006, John approached Gary Santone and Justin Broadbent in separate meetings. Gary was a jeweler from Philadelphia from whom John had bought Lauren's engagement ring. He was politically conservative and a rabid fan of the Three Stooges slapstick comedy routines. John had bought many, many pieces of jewelry from Gary over the years, and he referred to Gary and his wife Debbie as "very trustworthy people in a very slimy business." One night at dinner with Gary, John mentioned the easy money scam he was running at AIG. He told Gary that if he were willing to help him out, John would make it worth his while financially. He assured Gary there was no real risk to himself; John, as the AIG employee who was signing the checks, would be the one they'd come after if anybody ever got wise to it. Gary had heard enough. He was in.

John had met Justin Broadbent in a dive bar in Philadelphia, a place called the Medusa Lounge, one of several nightclubs that John owned in that city. Justin and a crew of his friends had sauntered in one morning before the bar was open; John had been sitting inside with Duffy, one of the bartenders who was getting the bar ready for the day shift. Justin and his entourage asked if they could get a beer, and John figured it couldn't hurt, so they had a beer. That beer turned into many, and the group stayed for several hours. From there, they all became regulars at the bar, and John got to know Justin very well. He was very skilled at Internet-related technologies, and he ended up designing the website for Medusa and, from there, he designed a website for Gary Santone's jewelry shop after John introduced them. When John offered him part of the action of his headhunting scheme, Justin had no reason to doubt John when he said that there was no risk involved for him. It was almost incestuous the way these relationships developed and co-mingled. And co-conspired.

And then there were three.

The first step in growing the scam was to get Santone and Broadbent set up with business names and the requisite tax identification numbers and all the other regulatory red tape they needed to get through in order to appear legitimate. John provided them with sample invoices just as he had with Tom, and explained how the process would work. It was simple, he assured them, because he was the one who would approve the payments to them, so there was no need to worry about getting caught as long as they kept to the guidelines John set forth. He told each of them that they would begin submitting invoices to him in January of the following year, and in the interim they would be setting up their companies and John would be adding them to the list of approved vendors so as to facilitate their getting paid. Additionally, they'd each be taken to lunch monthly so as to create the illusion of building a professional relationship. John had been through this before and he knew exactly what steps to take in order to make everything look above-board.

Tom, meanwhile, was continuing to submit invoices to John, who was continuing to pay them. They met once again at Il Vagabondo, and then back at the Palm the following month. Each lunch was expensed to AIG, as it should have been, and John left with an envelope with a check. The whole plan was working better than either of them could have ever dared hope. At their meeting at the Palm – it took place in November of that year – John told Tom about the fact that AIG didn't true-up the budget at year's end as long as there were invoices. What that meant for them, he went on to explain, was that the December invoices could be something of a Christmas bonus. All Tom needed to do was go heavy on the invoices, like he'd had an exceptionally busy month. It wasn't too far-fetched of an idea; the time around the holidays was a perfect time to go job seeking, so a headhunter might very well put in some extra hours in late November. And in reality, it didn't matter. John was approving the checks off the bench money fund account and there would be no reconciling of the budget to check for any discrepancies. So long as there was an invoice, nobody would even think twice about it.

Just before Christmas, John hosted a holiday stag party at a private club in Philadelphia. Justin Broadbent was one of the guests of honor, and if he'd had any doubts about John's sincerity before, those doubts were wiped clean when the "hired help" that John had brought in especially for that night gave Justin some extra special attention. Justin spent the night living like the rock star he wanted to be, and with John's help, that he would one day become, at least financially speaking. A few days later, John headed out to his home on

Nantucket with his family. They would celebrate the holidays on the little island thirty miles at sea.

As the year wound down inside the Tower, Christmas bonuses were handed around. Just before he was fired, Axel had gifted John a $200,000 bonus package. Edmund Tse had done well, bringing in around $15 million for the year, while Martin Sullivan took home about $20 million. Nottingham retired, pocketing about $5 million for the year and thirty years' worth of shares. All three had, of course, done quite well for themselves via Bermuda, as well.

Three days before Christmas, an envelope arrived via Federal Express at John's home on Nantucket. It was John's own Christmas bonus from Tom Pomboyno.

It had been a good year for everyone.

CHAPTER SIX
Covering Up Is Hard To Do

2007 began with a bang, as the atmosphere within the AIG Tower was growing increasingly anxious with regards to the Bermuda issue. With the hard stop on all payments from Bermuda in place, the issue of using the account was no longer an issue John had to concern himself with. However, the dark cloud hanging over the whole situation – namely, the fact that the practice had been going on for as long as anybody could actually remember – was cemented in place. The cloud was so firmly stuck in place due to the fact that it was approaching tax time, which meant that the time was drawing nigh when somebody was going to have to figure out how to weasel out of the collective mess that they'd managed to create for themselves. And things were about to go from sticky to downright stuck.

Anastasia Kelly brought in representatives from DL Piper, the firm that serves as AIG's outside counsel, and Ernst and Young, a national tax advising firm who was brought in to serve as an outside auditor. In essence, that means that AIG wanted to get both a legal and a fiscal opinion on what it had been doing. But they didn't want those opinions coming from its own regular advisors, but rather from a new firm that was somewhat more subject to AIG's control.

While most people understand the job of lawyers, the term "independent auditor" gets thrown around a lot in the business world, and a lot of people have no idea what it means. Basically an auditor is a person or group of people with a keen understanding of business practices, and it is their job to ensure that a company's records are accurate.

What made the choice of Ernst and Young so interesting to John was the fact that PriceWaterhouseCooper was AIG's normal auditor. Why, he asked himself, wasn't AIG using PWC? After all, they were the company most familiar with the Bermuda program, so it made sense that they would be the logical choice to serve as the ones to audit the books now that AIG was trying to clean up its act. But instead, AIG seemed to be specifically avoiding contact with PWC. It was actually a pretty elementary explanation that boiled down to the exact reason that they should have been called.

PriceWaterhouseCooper was the firm that knew the most about AIG's business records because they were AIG's independent auditor. And as a publicly traded company, AIG had to produce quarterly reports that detailed earnings-to-date, a report that was audited by PWC. AIG's fiscal year begins December 1, which meant that they'd already reported year-end earnings (in an audited report); their next reporting date would be March 1. They had three months from the date of their last report to clean this thing up, and if their true independent auditor found out what was going on, there was no telling what might happen once the Securities and Exchange Commission got involved. So it was DL Piper to the rescue, and the authorities at AIG began to work with DL Piper to develop their new reports on Bermuda.

John knew that both reports would come back with major problems for AIG and he could have told them that had they only asked his opinion, but corporate America doesn't work that way. It works by having groups pay other groups a lot of money in order to hear the "experts" say what is obvious to anybody. Rather than just using what you know — say, for instance, that failure to report hundreds of millions of dollars in taxable income is a violation of tax laws — you pay somebody else to tell you the same thing. But John played along anyway, providing information he was asked to provide to the various individuals who requested it. The point people for the whole operation, to nobody's surprise, were Rod Martin and Jackie Aguanno, with Martin Sullivan shadowing the whole thing from the sidelines.

In March, the first grenade of the new year fell into the foxhole.

Ordinarily, if you file your tax return on time, you're considered an upstanding individual who respects the system and understands that failure to file a return is oftentimes not the best way to approach your tax obligations. But when you're working on hiding taxable income, it's not a good idea to submit your return before everybody else involved in the cover-up has a chance to weigh-in on the subject.

So when John's phone rang in late March of that year and Rod Martin said he needed to talk to John about the Greek tax situation, John knew instantly what had happened. And the facts would bear out his initial gut instinct. The Greek office of ALICO had filed its return on March 15, 2007, for the taxes due for 2006. They'd been good citizens and filed their taxes a full month earlier than they were actually due. And they had been operating under the assumption that the Bermuda payments were legal, accepted and defendable in court, so they'd not included the entire tax liability for the year. That oversight might have lost them whatever points they might have amassed for filing early.

And then the emails started flying. On March 29, 2007, Merilyn Voulgareli, the assistant to Christos Mistilloglou, the Chief Operating Officer of the Greek office of ALICO, sent an email to George McClennen, Senior Vice President and Chief Financial Officer of ALICO. She said that, after reviewing the situation as it stood and discussing the issues with "Diomedes Vassiliou, the local H.R. people and the third party payroll administrator 'Accounting Solution' firm," she'd come to a series of conclusions about their situation:

- We cannot obtain an extension.

- The "book" of annual tax declaration for salaries has been actually filed on March 15th (copy of Summary first page attached).

- Filing today a revised tax declaration for salaries for 2006 is subject to local tax penalty for 2006.

- Any additional income tax declaration will also raise serious tax and accounting questions regarding the integrity/honesty of the local operation which has never been put in doubt since the incorporation/establishment of the Company in Greece (1964).

- Some of the people involved in the issue have already filed their 2006 personal income tax declaration which means that they need to file an adjusted one with the respective fines, etc.

- Finally, the executives affected have not received any income statement as of today from Home Office that will demonstrate the income to be declared, plus the taxes that should have been withheld and paid by the Company at source, as it is the law both in Greece and the United States.

- There are additional legal, tax, accounting and other complications, discussed with Diomedes and the others, which should be further analyzed and we are at your disposal to discuss.

The long and the short of this email was that the Greek office had jumped the gun on filing their tax information. But what made the whole situation so bizarre is that they'd previously been informed of the issues arising from the Bermuda account, and they'd just gone along doing things like they always had done them despite that fact. But now that they'd filed the information, the problems created by the past use of Bermuda were now exacerbated several times over, because now it was going to be even more difficult to explain what, exactly, was going on with the ALICO payment structures for some of its better paid executives. In other words, it's difficult to put the toothpaste back in the tube once you let it out. But why would they want to after all? The head of the Greek operation was getting a huge paycheck out of Bermuda, not to mention a Bermuda pension plan. What did he stand to gain by declaring it? In a sense, the Greek executives were forcing the home office's hand. It was a risky gambit to say the least.

That evening, after pow-wowing with several of his underlings, George McLennen forwarded the email he'd received from Greece to Holly Butler at DL Piper. His suggested "solution," for lack of a better term, was to submit the requisite payments to the authorities through a single payment by paying a lump sum settlement for all back taxes, interest and penalties, and hopefully not raise too many eyebrows at the same time:

> *Although in theory we could file an amended by tomorrow and still be on-time with respect to 2006 only (and given we did not yet know the penalty and interest dynamic arising for amendments lodged later than tomorrow, I say what follows with some caution), I think we should assess holistically what we owe Greece in totality and only amend or even approach the tax authority once we have a complete assessment made and overture to make.*

> *We don't yet know the statute of limitations and that would be helpful, but the optimal approach in my view is to take a holistic offer to the Greek authorities, for all unexpired/open periods and try to close the matter in one fell swoop (enveloping company and employee in that overture) rather than rush a one year amendment thru that could prompt reactions and questions that we are not wholly yet prepared to answer.*

We are not experts and of course are relying on you and E&Y for the technical matters, but at least Bruce, John and I have agreed this seems (absent further facts and in light of having already filed) to be the best way to go in order to protect ourselves and especially our key employees/managers, and not to create any divide or derision between company and employee/execs. (No implication meant therein you would in any way suggest that simply rather a concern that such could arise if the amendment drew immediate attention before we had our work done; Alico and Andreas personally have some high visibility within the Athens community).

We are of course at your disposal. Best regards!

There is a relatively obscure chess move called "en passant." The rule, introduced in 1490, allows for an unorthodox capture of a pawn by another pawn when a particular sequence of moves transpires. Briefly, if a player moves his pawn two spaces forward (as is allowable the first time a pawn is moved from its starting row) and his opponent could have captured it had he only moved it one square, the opponent is entitled to capture the pawn as if it had moved only one square, provided that the capture is executed on the very next move after the original pawn had moved. In the case of Vassilliou, he held his position and made a move that caught the home office by surprise. By doing so, he had locked in the fact that he wouldn't be forced by Rod Martin or George McClennen to report the income that he and several of his top chieftains were receiving via the Bermuda entity. It was part and parcel of the culture of greed fostered by the firm worldwide.

In the end, Rod blinked, so Diomedes pounced. Checkmate.

The damage had been done and now it was time to start doing what they could to contain that damage. At this point, the options were severely limited. There was a chance the Greeks could get away with it, simply because the Bermuda office was notorious for failing to send correct paperwork. George

Dove was the Vice President who oversaw operations for American International Companies (AICO), which was one of the shells AIG maintained. AICO's basic purpose was to process payroll for expatriate employees of AIG living abroad. Its more sinister purpose was to help expats avoid certain taxes, with a degree of dubious regard for all of the legal niceties mixed in.

Dove is a big man of Bermudian ancestry – the Bermudian employment laws are very good at protecting jobs for native Bermudians over expats. His accent sounds more Jamaican than Bermudian, and he was basically a low-level operative who did what he was told by his immediate boss, namely Jackie Aguanno.

Dove's claim to fame was his ability to screw up payroll procedures, which was one of his character flaws that some ALICO execs were hoping to cash in on to avoid any trouble in regards to the Greek situation. Dove and his assistants processed over 400 employee payroll records manually every month, and John said that "not a month went by when we didn't get a call from somewhere in the world that their Bermuda pay wasn't right, and we got many, many calls about Bermuda pay not showing up at all." John referred to the operation as "an administrative abortion."

Capitalizing on the fact that Dove seemed less-than-capable at getting the right pay to the right people, Jackie Aguanno and Rod Martin asked him to issue an "earnings statement" for the Greek office; they asked him to go ahead and back-date it, too, just for good measure. The suggestion was that he'd forgotten to do it, which, given his history, would not sound completely implausible. They were asking for Dove to issue a W-2; Dove didn't quite get the message properly, however, and instead wrote a two-line letter on letterhead from the AIG Bermuda headquarters. John found out later that when the Greeks had received this "official document," they'd had a good laugh about it before throwing it in the trash. During that same conversation, John also learned that the Greek office had intentionally filed their tax returns early so as to prevent any intervention by McClennen. They'd been one step ahead of the home office all along.

By April of 2007, things had calmed down as the crisis seemed to have passed, at least temporarily. But the executives at AIG weren't going to rest on any laurels they might have had lying around. They were still in full-on cover-up mode. John met with Martin Sullivan, among other members of the senior leadership team, to discuss what could be done about the Bermuda problem. It seemed to be, at this point, a foregone conclusion that most illegal payments off the Bermuda account were a thing of the past, though John figured that more than one former recipient of Bermuda payments would find a way to continue getting them, despite the hard stop.

But the whole situation had turned into something like the world's biggest golf ball. If you cut the plastic off a golf ball, you'll see that inside is a small rubber ball with a very long elastic thread wrapped tightly around it. If you cut that elastic, the whole thing unwinds like a tornado in reverse. The trick is to find the end of the elastic and detach it, so that you can unwind it at your own speed.

It was the same thing with the Bermuda operations. They'd cut off the white cover; now it was time to see if they could find where the elastic was glued down to itself so that they could undo it and start unwinding the mess at a reasonable pace that they could control. Because if they cut the elastic, it was not going to end well for anybody involved.

By now, though, John had bigger issues to contend with. The Securities and Exchange Commission had announced in April that they would be sending an independent counsel to conduct a routine investigation of all of AIG's international operations. It was an unfortunate coincidence that had nothing to do with Bermuda, but nobody knew that at the time. Given the timing, there were a lot of nervous people walking the halls at 70 Pine Street.

In reality, it was simply a compliance investigation that the SEC was conducting. They wanted to look into deficiencies at AIG, areas where the company needed to focus its efforts on improving in both process and procedure. But again, nobody within the corporate hierarchy of AIG knew exactly what the purpose was, so it was deemed that it was better to be safe than sorry. An order came down from Rod Martin, Edmund Tse and Anastasia Kelly that nobody was to mention Bermuda. And just to be absolutely sure that there was no question about who would be saying what, John and other executives were prepped in one-on-one meetings with Steve Gorman and later with Anastasia Kelly.

Gorman told John that he was not to bring up the subject of Bermuda at all, no matter what. Don't mention it, don't allude to it, don't talk about it. He explained to John that if the SEC investigator brought up Bermuda, John was to play dumb. He was to say that he really didn't know anything about it. He'd never been to Bermuda, he'd never met George Dove, he knew nothing about the operations there and he didn't feel comfortable talking about it due to his lack of knowledge. Anything about Bermuda was to be directed to Gorman himself. All of this, of course, flew in the face of the truth. John had met George Dove on countless occasions, had spoken with him on the phone hundreds of times and had exchanged dozens of emails with him. But he would be the good soldier and obey orders.

Then it was Anastasia Kelly's turn with him. She echoed, almost verbatim, what Steve had told him to say, though she was more veiled in how she said it. "All you need to say," she explained, "is that it's not your area, they don't report to you, you haven't been there and you don't know any of those people. It's best for everyone if we just don't mention it until we get it fixed." John knew that this was an absolute sin of omission. The SEC independent counsel focused on compliance issues, and for them to omit any mention of Bermuda bordered on high treason.

When it came time to speak to the investigator, John did exactly as he'd been instructed, despite the fact that his own conscience was having conflicts with his actions. As much of a scammer as he had been — and continued to be, for that matter — this was different. This was the SEC. This was the public's trust. This was Bernie Madoff before Bernie made headlines. And this was a little late to be claiming problems arising from a troubled conscience.

In his interview with the SEC independent counsel, John was straightforward and truthful with the questions that were asked of him. He spent about an hour talking about global policy and procedures, which focused especially on the compliance and regulatory training that John's HR staff received. He stuck to his orders of not veering off into territory that he was not deemed an expert in, such as the topic of Bermuda. And despite assurances from his superiors at the firm that he'd have AIG representation in the meeting, such was not the case. It was just John, the SEC investigator and a representative from DL Piper who sat silently and took notes. In fact, when John asked him if he was in the room as a legal representative, the DL Piper representative told John that he was on his own, because he would not be serving in the capacity of his attorney. He learned later that every other person they'd spoken to had been afforded the presence of an AIG representative. At that point, he knew for sure that he had been set afloat on AIG's version of the Raft of Medusa.

There were some occasional questions that caused John to fall back on his rehearsed defense lines about how he wasn't familiar with that area and it would be better if he asked the question of whomever else he could think of to pass the buck to. Looking back on the meeting, what struck John most about the whole thing was that the questions were limited solely to domestic issues. AIG had offices around the world, and one of the things that made it so easy for them to cover their tracks was the fact that it seemed like nothing was ever done the same way in multiple countries. Bonus structures were different across the different countries, payroll systems were different, reporting processes, hiring, firing, product management, all of it. Everything was done differently in different countries, and AIG ran roughshod over laws in so many of those foreign countries.

Yet the SEC had no interest in finding out anything about that; their only concern was how the operations in the United States were going. And for what it's worth, they weren't even terribly effective in rooting out wrongdoing there, either, given the fact that the factors that led to the company's financial collapse were already in place, just waiting for the fuse to burn down enough for them to explode.

When the time came for DL Piper to present its assessment of the Bermuda situation, the meeting was attended by what John called "a true brotherhood of thieves" that included Martin, Aguanno, Tse, Kelly, Kaslow (who had replaced Axel Freudmann) and a collection of what John described as "black-bag operatives from DL Piper." It was yet another in the long series of experts telling people what they already knew to be true, but who were hoping against hope that they were wrong. It turns out they were right, though. But they'd bought themselves a good legal team that was able to craft a report that tried its best to minimize the damage.

The report itself never left the conference room, but John was able to read it after it was back-channeled to him by his own "Deep Throat" who had attended the meeting. John himself had been cut from the guest list. As he read it, he found himself at times biting his lower lip in order to keep from laughing out loud at some of the report's "findings."

One such "finding" that he thought was particularly comical was the classification of the Bermuda payroll scheme as "a forty-year-old payroll practice" that was deemed "outdated" and in need of "modernization." Nowhere was there any mention of the fact that the practice had long ago been deemed illegal and suspended, only to be resurrected by certain individuals and then covered up when discovered. It reminded John of *The Wizard of Oz.* Whoever had prepared the presentation was only allowing the viewing public to see what DL Piper and AIG wanted them to see. Dorothy saw only a company that was working diligently to correct problems associated with an "outdated" method of distributing wealth. John saw himself as Toto, whose job it was to pull back the curtain and expose the "great and powerful" for what it really was, an illegal tax dodge spread out over half the globe.

In August of that year, the decision was made, after careful consideration and much heated debate by all involved, that in order to resolve the Bermuda tax issues, AIG would take tax amnesty where it was available to them and "avoid disclosing" the information in what were deemed "high-risk" countries. What that amounted to was that AIG was willing to pay for their tax-related sins, but only to a certain point. In countries where they wouldn't be able to get out with just a single lump settlement payment – places like France, Dubai, Hong Kong and Greece – they were going to stick to the party line and deny, deny, deny. The statute of limitations is different in each country, however, so there was no telling how long they'd have to keep up the subterfuge. In other words, pray like hell that your duck-and-cover maneuver is enough to protect you from the atomic blast that's about to go off right next to you.

Case in point, Title 26, Section 6501 of the United States Tax code states:

Except as otherwise provided in this section, the amount of any tax imposed by this title shall be assessed within 3 years after the return was filed (whether or not such return was filed on or after the date prescribed) or, if the tax is payable by stamp, at any time after such tax became due and before the expiration of 3 years after the date on which any part of such tax was paid, and no proceeding in court without assessment for the collection of such tax shall be begun after the expiration of such period. For purposes of this chapter, the term "return" means the return required to be filed by the taxpayer (and does not include a return of any person from whom the taxpayer has received an item of income, gain, loss, deduction, or credit).

What that is telling you is that the IRS has three years to come after you once you've filed your return. This is why, as a general rule, many people will tell you that you have to keep copies of your tax returns for three years. That's the statute of limitations on taxes in the United States, and most foreign countries have their own version of varying statutes of limitations in regards to income tax evasion that sound about the same. In the case of the US, though, it's basically no audits after three years. But nothing about AIG or the tax code is "basic," or so it seems.

In the case of the US tax code, there are ten exceptions listed to the "General Rule" that gives the IRS three years to come after you. Among those exceptions are things like excise taxes, gift taxes, granted extensions and that sort of thing. And then there are the exceptions for situations like "a false or fraudulent return with the intent to evade tax" or "a willful attempt in any manner to defeat or evade tax imposed by this title." In those instances, there is no statute of limitations. In other words, if the IRS can prove that an entity knowingly submitted false returns, they can audit that entity — be it an individual or a corporation — at any time in that entity's existence. And, in fact, there are more than a few corpses that have had their estates audited despite the overt lack of vital signs exhibited by the would-be taxpayer. Thus, despite the inevitability of both death and taxes, it would seem from that example that the former does not necessarily prevent the latter.

Only time will tell if the inevitability of taxes proves true in the case of AIG.

*   *   *

The plan for 2007 was for John and Tom Pomboyno to bill AIG for $40,000 a month for headhunting services, of which John would get a cut. It was a lot of money they were talking about, but it wasn't so big that John was worried it might get caught in any internal auditing designed to catch financial abnormalities. And since John was overseeing the whole department responsible for paying Tom and others like him, he figured they were pretty safe.

Gary and Justin were another matter altogether, however. Because they were new to the system, John thought it was best to bring them along gradually in terms of the amount of money they would be billing. If everyone played their cards right in this whole operation, they could all get very wealthy very quickly, and all without doing a whole lot work. It was just a matter of being patient. The start-up issues were difficult, especially with Gary's business name. For whatever reason, when he was input as a new vendor into the HR system, the business name was refused. On the magical third time around, though, everything went smoothly and both were officially on the AIG list of approved vendors and able to serve as corporate headhunters for the firm.

In February of 2007, both Gary and Justin had submitted their first set of invoices. They'd been practicing with John for the month prior, using sample invoices that John provided for them to use as a template, the same as he'd done for Tom. So when the time came for the first round of invoices to be processed, they were old pros and nobody was too worried about whether or not they'd make it through the system with ease. By this point, even John had

150

lost any sense of nervousness he'd had in the past. The successes he'd had with Tom up to now had lulled him into a sense of security that made the whole operation feel almost normal and legal. Things were busy in February for John, as he was neck-deep in working on the Bermuda cover-up, so he and Tom skipped their monthly lunch-and-money-transfer meeting; instead, Tom just put a check in a FedEx envelope and mailed it to John.

The invoices all slid through the processing system without a hesitation, and all three co-conspirators got checks for their services. Both Gary and Justin were so blown away by how easy the whole thing had been that they couldn't believe it. They both agreed to do another round of invoices, which John would process in the same way. That month, John went to Sparks Steakhouse with Tom, where the two made toasts to their good fortune and the financial killing they were making off of AIG. "We're just like Big Pauly," John said, referring to the infamous head of the Gambino crime family who was once referred to as "the Howard Hughes of the Mob." The reference was a chillingly accurate foretelling. Big Pauly, who was arrested on charges of racketeering in 1985 and released on bail awaiting trial, was killed, together with his bodyguard, on what were allegedly direct orders from John Gotti on December 16.

Big Pauly was gunned down outside of Sparks Steakhouse.

The next month, things again went smoothly for all three of the bogus headhunters. They submitted their invoices right on schedule and the checks were written and sent to them. They in turn cashed those checks and rendered unto John that which was John's. Gary made the trip to John's office to hand-deliver his check, while Justin sent his payment via FedEx. Tom, as had become almost habit, met with John over food, this time for dinner at Smith & Wollensky. The money kept rolling in and AIG kept picking up the tab for their meals, so there was nothing the pair could find to complain about as they lingered over expensive red wine and porterhouse steaks.

By May, the furthest thing from John's mind was the idea that the scam he'd so artfully put together would be coming to a relatively quick ending. He didn't have any sense of impending doom, no vision of clouds on the horizon. All he was seeing was dollar signs, despite the legal wrangling he was going through in his "other" life at AIG. By now, he looked at the time he spent working with his co-conspirators as almost a break from the bigger conspiracy that he was engaged in at his office.

Perhaps Gary sensed something. Nobody can say for sure, not even Gary. But for whatever reason, Gary decided that May was the month when he needed extra cash, so he proposed a rather daring move. He would send in invoices for the month of May that would basically exhaust the amount of money John had budgeted for his yearly payout. It would be a big payday for Gary — assuming nothing caught the exponential increase in the amount due — and, in turn, a big payday for John. Falcetta agreed to the plan, and then went to meet with Justin. He and Justin confirmed their plan that Justin would submit the standard invoice amount for July. John met Tom Pomboyno later that month for yet another lunch meeting, and the pair confirmed that Tom, too, would be submitting his standard invoices. Everything was in place for the following month, and John could rest easy, knowing that the scam was going forward as planned.

And everything did go as planned. All three men got their checks — even Gary's big one that had caused more than a little anxiety for both Gary and John — and John got his payments, all via FedEx delivery.

And then the wheels all fell off simultaneously.

"It has become apparent that one of the central causes of the financial and economic crises we face today is the widespread failure of governance."
—Senator Charles Schumer

CHAPTER SEVEN
Black and White and Sometimes Grey

Global income tax evasion and the occasional gratuitous payment to non-working headhunters weren't the only eyebrow-raising activities being engaged in by executives at the highest levels of AIG's Life Insurance division known as ALICO. No, there were more than enough scams to go around the Tower of Thieves a few times over. And they varied as to their degree of creativity and legality. One of these questionable business activities that was engaged in by the AIG Life Insurance division was what was openly referred to as "grey market" activities in Latin America. Openly, at least, within the safe confines of company memoranda and conversations.

In September of 2005, John attended the annual strategy meeting of ALICO, which was held that year in London, England. At the meeting, executives from all divisions within the company presented business performance reports relating to their respective divisions over the course of three days. The basic topics that most of the presentations concerned themselves with were things like budgets and business goals for the upcoming year and topics of that nature. Fascinating stuff, to be sure, but it was another presentation that sparked John Falcetta's curiosity at this particular annual meeting. During a review relating to international businesses, a rather lively debate arose around the appropriateness of the "grey market" operations that AIG was conducting in, among other places, the country of Panama. Additional operations were servicing Brazil, Peru, Chile and Columbia, all working through the Panama office.

A grey market can be thought of as a black market's timid cousin.

They're not quite as morally reprehensible or as dangerous or as illegal, but those who participate in grey market activities are certainly tiptoeing around the edge of a deep hole, and if they aren't careful, they'll fall all the way down to the levels of the black markets.

To put it in more definitive terms, a black market operation is strictly illegal; something like selling and receiving stolen artifacts would be black market activity. Grey markets, however, are not expressly illegal; they are, however, closer to being illegal than they are to being legal. Basically a grey market operation is one that takes a legal commodity – say, for example, an insurance policy – and markets it through distribution channels that are not the originally intended channels for that specific commodity. These channels are typically loosely-regulated or unauthorized. In other words, it's a secretive kind of transaction.

Again, it's important to understand that there is nothing expressly illegal about grey market operations. Grey markets exist quite openly for things like wine, pharmaceuticals and automobiles. In the case of cars, it's not uncommon in European countries for a resident of one country to travel to another to purchase a new vehicle in order to avoid things like higher tax rates in their home countries. Similarly, there is a very profitable market in the exporting of used vehicles from Japan to countries around the world. Both are instances of grey market activities, because the cars are being purchased through channels that aren't necessarily the ones originally intended by the car manufacturers or the government regulators.

AIG, however, wasn't in the wine or car grey market. They were, instead, operating in what they knew, namely insurance. And given ALICO's attachment to life insurance specifically, it should come as no surprise that the specific commodity in question for this grey market activity was life insurance policies. In short, AIG had discovered a mother lode of customers doing business from Latin American countries, customers who were buying up life insurance policies like they were going out of style. After a period of time, the policies were cancelled. But then, interestingly enough, oftentimes the same customer would buy another life insurance policy soon after cancelling the first one.

After the discussion of the activities as they related to AIG's business practices, John sought out an explanation as to what exactly the company was doing. He learned, through the course of that investigation, that Dan Costello, a Vice President for Account Management, headed up the operation. Costello, in turn, reported directly to JoAnne Warren, Senior Vice President and Chief Accounting Officer for ALICO. Under these two top executives was a team of approximately twenty people in Panama who reported to Raquel Gonzalez, who at the time was in the Wilmington, Delaware, offices of AIG. In what should surprise exactly nobody at this point, Ms. Gonzalez reported directly to Messrs. Sullivan and Martin in the AIG Tower in Manhattan.

John inquired as to how lucrative the life insurance market was in Panama and whether or not said market justified a team of twenty employees with three executives overseeing the operations. He posed the question to each of the three executives – Costello, Warren and Gonzalez – and in each case got three different answers, which taken together led him to believe that there was something the trio was trying to hide. The only point that they could seem to agree on was that the majority of the money that paid for the policies was thought to be cash that had come from brokers in Latin America. There wasn't any definitive discussion about the origin of the money; "Latin America" was the only common descriptor the three managed to come up with. Regardless of origin, that Latin American money was being used to purchase life insurance policies from AIG in Panama, and each of those policies was denominated in US dollars, despite the fact that they were paid for in foreign currency.

The way it would work was something like this: A respected broker in Panama might make application for an insurance policy on behalf of another person or company, a person we'll call Mr. Columbia, just for simplicity's sake. Mr. Columbia then makes payment to his businessman friend, who in turn deposits Mr. Columbia's money into a local bank account. The businessman then requests that the bank send a wire transfer to AIG so as to pay for Mr. Columbia's insurance policy. From there, ALICO, working on behalf of AIG, issues the policy for Mr. Columbia. So now we have Mr. Columbia, occupation unknown, who has sent money of unknown origin to an American insurance company through a third party, despite the fact that he himself is Columbian and it might make a lot more sense for Mr. Columbia to choose AIG's Columbian insurance company as opposed to the New York company, but that's just not how he rolls.

When John spoke with Costello about this issue, in fact, Costello told him that there were similar policies available locally throughout Latin America. So in other words, the Columbian could just get a policy from the local offices in Columbia. That begged the question, at least in John's mind, as to why a person would bother sending money through a third party (or even a fourth party) all the way to Panama for the same policy he could get locally. The question was a rhetorical one. And it was also one for which Mr. Costello was unable to provide an answer to John.

On the surface, though, the whole thing seems pretty benign. Some people like to spend money in odd ways. Whereas one guy might buy a two-hundred-foot yacht, some other guy wants to buy an insurance policy from a foreign country, despite the fact that he could buy more-or-less the same policy locally with a whole lot less hassle. Who knows why? More importantly, who cares? After all, it's his money and he's entitled to spend it however he wants to, no matter how odd you or I might think it is.

And speaking of money, what's with all this talk about how he makes his money? What's the relevance? Maybe the guy's a car dealer. Maybe he's a coke dealer. Does it really matter? If we're going to assume he's trafficking cocaine simply because of the fact that he's Columbian, isn't that racial profiling at its absolute worst? All things considered, he's a human being, he needs insurance and AIG is in the business of selling insurance. It's none of their business how the guy in question makes his money, so AIG isn't going to go sticking its corporate nose into that sort of matter.

International legal opinions on this type of business transaction are sketchy at best. On the one hand, it's no business of anybody's at AIG how some businessman — be he a banana grower or a fisherman or whatever else — came to be in possession of massive amounts of cash. They can always fall back on the fact that maybe he's just that good at growing bananas or catching fish or whatever else. But there is a legal term — "willful blindness" — that describes what might be termed the other side of the story.

"Willful blindness" is exactly what it sounds like, namely the intentional act of not seeing. It is sometimes called "willful ignorance" or "contrived ignorance," but no matter what you call it, it's a defense based on the idea that somebody didn't know that what they were doing was in any way connected to an illegal act. One recent court case that examined this issue involved AIMster, which was a close relative of the music file sharing software called Napster, the company that made headlines in 2001 by facilitating illegal file sharing. The AIMster gang claimed that they had no way of monitoring what their users were doing, thus it wasn't their fault if their users were illegally sharing files.

The United States Court of Appeals for the Seventh Circuit disagreed and found them liable, because they should have known what could reasonably be expected to result from what their users were doing with files. In other words, if there's an obvious reason people are using your product — and that obvious reason is to commit illegal acts – then you can't fall back on the defense that you had no idea that people were going to use your product to do what they were doing.

Legal issues aside, it doesn't – or at least it shouldn't – take a Mensa membership certificate to surmise that a person in a country that is known for drug money who is utilizing a third party in order to purchase an insurance policy that is itself redeemable for cash after a certain period of time is possibly trying to hide the source of his income. And why would he possibly be trying to hide his source of income? Drug money is "dirty" money; it's liable to seizure by government officials who are seeking some good press by cracking down on drug dealers. And while he could just invest it in a more traditional manner and then cash in his investment, any sort of expenditure of cash of that amount is going to raise a few eyebrows when it is suddenly injected into the local economies.

So he sends his dirty money to AIG and gets his clean insurance policy. And once that money has gone through the bank to AIG and back again once the original Mr. Columbia cashes in his policy, that money is as clean as the driven snow. It's come from a reputable source – AIG – and that reputable source has a pretty hard paper trail that it can use to show that the insurance policy was issued after receipt of a wire transfer from an equally reputable source in Panama. So what was once dirty money is now clean.

That's why they call it money laundering.

And it's not just bankers who are engaged in this sort of thing. It's not uncommon in that part of the world for a local merchant – be it a store owner or a fisherman or a legitimate farmer – to serve as a front for those whose income is generated from other less legal "cash crops." The most important part of the scheme, regardless of who serves as the front, is that there is a level of separation between the origin of the money itself and the issuer of the policy. The more levels of separation, the better.

So certain elements of AIG were engaging in this grey market money laundering, either knowingly or not. Of course if the participants were actively engaging in this activity with a full and complete understanding of what it was they were doing, they'd be considered co-conspirators engaged in the crime of money laundering. But because they can claim blissful ignorance, they're legally clear of any wrongdoing. They can at least until somebody starts sniffing around and figures out that what they're doing is in fact willfully blinding themselves to the fact that they're laundering drug money. In fact, as recently as late 2006 and early 2007, Brazilian authorities maintained an open file on AIG and potential money laundering activities the company was engaged in there.

One of the core elements of any prosecution involves motive. Motive is not a requirement for a prosecution – those who seek to put somebody behind bars are under no obligation to prove motive at all – but it certainly helps to show why somebody would do something as a precursor to trying to prove that they did it in the first place. So why would a multi-national, multi-billion dollar company like AIG engage in behavior like this? What was there for them to gain by issuing insurance policies that were cancelled as soon as possible by the purchasers after they were issued?

Money, plain and simple.

These policies are much like Certificates of Deposit at a bank in that there is a "substantial penalty for early withdrawal." AIG issues policies that offer the purchaser a chance to cancel at any time, but there's a hefty fee for doing so. So if you drop a thousand dollars to buy a policy and then change your mind a month later, they'll let you do that. They'll cancel your policy and refund your money, less an early cancellation fee that can go by any of hundreds of different names. That amount can be anywhere from ten-percent on up.

Let's take the example of our Columbian entrepreneur again. If he is in fact selling cocaine, he's probably got a pretty serious chunk of change he's trying to clean, so maybe he's buying a million dollar policy. He gives his million dollars to some fisherman who takes it to a bank who wires it to AIG. AIG – again, in its state of blissful ignorance – issues an insurance policy to a Columbian fisherman. After a year or so, that fisherman decides he doesn't really need as much insurance as he thought he did, so he decides to cancel the policy, which he's legally allowed to do under the terms of the policy. He cancels it and requests a refund. AIG sends him a check, but that check might only be for $900,000.

AIG deducts their cut – in this case, we're using a 10% early termination fee – and sends the remainder back to the fisherman. So he's got $900,000, and maybe he gets to keep $20,000 of it for his troubles. So our original Mr. Columbia, the guy who started this whole process, now has $880,000 US, all of which is totally clean and free of any drug association, and all of which he can safely stash in an offshore Panamanian bank account, where it will be safe from any local authorities or governmental intervention. Nobody at AIG "knowingly" did anything illegal; as far as they're concerned, they're helping a Panamanian fisherman keep his family safe in the event of his untimely demise, which, fortunately for all involved, never came to pass. And with operations in Panama, Chile, Peru and several other Latin American countries known to be sources for drug money, the product, the infrastructure and the profit motive are all present.

Of course, it's possible that Panama is such a lucrative place, from an insurer's perspective, because you've got so many people there who have these momentary flights of concern that they're at risk of losing their lives and so they take out very expensive (and refundable) insurance policies but then decide that they don't need them after all once they've held on to them for a little while. Yes, that's possible. It's just a matter of how willfully blind you care to be.

CHAPTER EIGHT
What the Shareholders Don't Know
Won't Hurt Them

AIG is a publicly traded company, and its stock is traded on the New York Stock Exchange. That means that the company's overall value is determined in large part by the stock price on a given day, which is in turn determined by the sentiments of investors. If they feel that the company's stock is worth more than it is currently selling for, they buy more of it, which tends to drive the price up. Alternatively, if investors feel the company is overvalued, they will sell, thus driving the stock price down. One of the main factors that drives the decision in the minds of investors as to whether to buy or sell is information that is released from the company itself. Most of that information is financial related – things like 10K forms and financial statements; typically good news results in a jump in the stock price, whereas negative news more often than not results in a dip in the stock's price as investors sell it.

In the case of a publicly traded company like AIG, the shareholders truly are the owners of the company. A share of stock, though a fractional piece, is a piece of ownership in the company. And all of those stockholders, no matter how large or small their respective positions in AIG stock, all have a vested interest in the company's success. If something were going on behind closed doors that was to somehow negatively impact the company's earnings at the expense of shareholders – and without their knowledge – then that action would qualify as shareholder abuse, because it could have a direct bearing on the company's earnings and thus the value of the company.

In many cases, what qualifies as shareholder abuse might not seem, on the surface, to be that major a deal. For example, a secretary who leaves early but manipulates her time card to indicate that she'd actually spent more time in the office than she really had is technically stealing from the company, right? Of course, she's probably not getting away with that much money, so it's probably not that big a deal. Unless a single secretary is able to pocket over $20,000 annually that she didn't really earn. Then it might be a little bigger deal. And, using the old adage about cockroaches – that where you see one, there are many more hiding behind the walls that you don't see – it's not too much of a stretch of the human imagination to think that there are multiple secretaries doing the identical thing.

Case in point, as the one in charge of Human Resources at AIG's largest global division, John was well acquainted with some lower level scams that rivaled the Bermuda payroll scheme for sheer brashness. One scam was perpetrated by at least one secretary working in the Tower that resulted in her making over $20,000 unearned. Her boss was required to approve all of her timecards weekly; he wasn't much for working on Fridays, so on Thursday at around noon, before he left early for the weekend, he'd sign her timecard for the week. Nobody said anything about the fact that he was leaving the office early so as to better enjoy a three-and-a-half-day weekend every week; after all, he's on salary, and it's nobody's business how many hours he works every week. But those time card people better make sure they keep their hours right.

Once it was signed, she didn't need to do anything else but fill in the times she was "at work." Once her boss left the office, his secretary was out the door soon after. She'd come in some time late on Friday and turn in her time-card, with the result being that she got paid for a day-and-a-half of work that she never actually performed. She bilked the company for $20,000 a year. And remember those cockroaches. That $20,000 was the one John saw in the kitchen when he turned on the lights one night. There's no telling how many secretaries were stealing in the exact same way across all the divisions of AIG. John's own estimate as to the amount of money spent on "lost time" wages for the Tower at 70 Pine Street alone topped $10 million in total.

Another scam that John happened upon at AIG was what he affectionately referred to as the "Back-to-School Scam." Several of the secretaries at ALICO were granted the authority to buy supplies for the office, both in terms of things like printer cartridges and legal pads for the supply closet, and things like bottled water and snacks for the break room. At one point around August, however, John noticed a spike in both the orders for supplies and one particular secretary's request for Saturday overtime hours, not to mention the car service she was billing to the office to get her there every Saturday. Ironically, John told me that if she'd just taken a cab instead of a car service, she probably would have gotten away with the whole thing.

This particular secretary was at the Tower every Saturday morning like clockwork, at her desk, by about nine-thirty or ten o'clock in the morning, and she'd stay for four or five hours every Saturday for a few weeks in late August and early September. While most bosses would appreciate the dedication of an employee willing to sacrifice their Saturdays for the company, as it turned out, this particular secretary wasn't quite so dedicated to her job as her attendance might have suggested. She was actually selling all of the supplies she was ordering, and pocketing the profits. Her customer base consisted solely of parents seeking to save money on back-to-school supplies, things like pens and paper and that sort of thing. And she expanded her operation to foodstuffs, too, adding in bottled water, juice, tea, whatever might have been ordered for the offices. Then came the orders for small file cabinets, desk chairs, printers. You name it, if it came out of an office supply catalog, she could get it for you.

In other words, she was serving as an expensive wholesaler, ordering the sort of things that would have been put in the supply closet for the AIG employees and the office break rooms, not to mention the equipment she would occasionally order for the offices themselves. And she was making a killing off selling those office supplies. Office supplies that AIG was paying for. Or, perhaps more exactly, office supplies that AIG's shareholders were paying for. Money was literally walking out the door of the retail outlet operating on Saturdays at 70 Pine Street.

To top it off, she also offered home delivery, for an extra fee, of course. Home delivery was a popular option for many of her clients, because parking in the Financial District, even on a Saturday morning, can be next-to-impossible. The saleswoman made a tidy profit off deliveries, especially given that she was billing AIG for the car service she used to transport the goods to their final destinations.

And then there was the "I Don't Need No Stinkin' Raise Scam" that, according to John, dozens of lower level management employees ran. Many employees in this category were responsible for submitting time sheets on behalf of their departments, which included themselves. And much as John himself signed off on HR checks that went for fruitless labors, so, too, did many of these managers. Because they were the ones in charge of the time sheets, they could approve overtime. Which meant that they could approve their own overtime, too.

So when several members of this group of lower ranking managers asked for and were subsequently denied a raise, it wasn't uncommon for them to take fiscal matters into their own hands and grant themselves overtime, hours that they may or may not have worked and, quite frankly, hours that they may or may not have approved had someone else asked for them. Each of these employees, by "working" time-and-a-half, was capable of pocketing upwards of $30,000 annually in overtime alone. John's own overtime analysis – which was weighted for both real and probable overtime – estimated a loss to the company of approximately $10 million every year.

And the further up the corporate ladder you went, the bigger the scams got. Case in point, the AIG relocation program (which, despite its suggestions of wartime refugees, was actually a pretty mundane program for helping employees move from one city to another when they'd gotten transferred) made it a policy specifically not to buy houses for or from employees. They'd help to pay your moving-related expenses, but selling your existing home and buying a new one in your new location was totally between you and whatever real estate agent you chose to hire.

But when David Fravel, Executive Vice President in charge of Strategic Planning and Solutions Services at AIG, was relocating, his good buddy Rod Martin took it upon himself to help him out. Rod told David that AIG would guarantee the purchase of his house, so if he couldn't sell it, AIG would buy it from him at the asking price. The house, which was valued at about $1.9 million, was listed for sale at $2.4 million. Fravel apparently figured that he'd like to turn a pretty decent profit on this sale, so he considered the appraised value as a low-ball offer. And given that he wasn't the low-ball kind of guy, he went ahead and asked for more. After all, he had nothing to lose, given that AIG was going to buy it for the appraised value. So there was nowhere for him to go but up.

A Heaven-sent savior appeared on the scene for AIG, one who would save them from having to fork out almost two million dollars for a house that nobody needed. A buyer appeared and offered Fravel $2.1 million, which, though lower than the asking price, was well above the negotiated value and would have been a gift of epic proportions to anybody else. Fravel, however, got greedy. He figured that if there was somebody willing to pay that much, he'd surely be able to find somebody who would pay his full asking price.

The house stayed on the market for a few months longer, and Fravel finally went to Martin and told him that it was time for AIG to make good on their promise. With that, AIG was on the hook for the purchase price of $1.9 million. Of course, they did have the opportunity to sell the house and take whatever money they could get from it. But the rest, as they say, is housing market slump history. Thank you, AIG shareholders, from the bottom of David Fravel's heart. Fortunately for you, though, AIG did manage to sell the house in the end, though at a loss of $200,000.

As the head of HR, John oversaw a lot of employees who worked in the AIG Tower in New York. And according to payroll records, a lot of those employees had what sounded like one horrendous commute. One employee in question actually lived in Detroit, Michigan, yet somehow made it to work everyday in Manhattan. And despite the fact that he had to travel over six-hundred miles each way, this mystery employee never missed a day of work.

And what's more, John never met the person in question, despite the fact that the mystery employee supposedly worked directly under him and reported to Rod Martin. Oftentimes these "employees" were the ne'er do well children of officials in countries where AIG either hoped to get some sort of sweetheart deal or, alternatively, the equally ne'er do well children of businessmen that had "done a lot" for good ol' AIG. All told, these "no-show" jobs cost AIG between four and five million dollars annually in New York alone; the global number could have easily eclipsed the $20 million-per-year mark. These payments were recorded in the overall budget, but very few shareholders were privy to the fact that the employees weren't actually doing anything to earn their paychecks.

Speaking of no-show jobs, there was another unreported fiasco that struck the payroll department in Wilmington, Delaware, at the ALICO headquarters there. John noticed at one point that the ALICO payroll account was seeing a lot of errors. "The Line," as it's called in business parlance, is a benchmark standard that, once exceeded, means that there is clearly an accounting problem that needs to be addressed due to more money going out than there should be.

John began investigating why the payroll budget for the Wilmington office seemed to be so far off the mark every month. It was almost as if several people were getting paid twice every month, but that didn't make any sense to him. So he looked and he looked and he looked. And the more John examined the situation, the more obvious it became to him that there was a situation in Delaware whereby employees were getting paid twice for the same pay period – one would be a direct-deposit payment, the other a hard-copy check issued off the payroll account and mailed to the employee. One employee, one pay period, two checks, both of them cashed. And it kept happening, month after month. Always different employees, but the same thing. One employee would get his or her direct deposit as normal, but then they'd also get a hard-copy check mailed to them. It was sloppy payroll work, to be sure. Or was it?

The closer he looked, the more convinced he was that it was an inside job.

As it turned out, there were a few employees in the payroll department who were masterminding this scam. When the employees in question received their checks in the mail, they dutifully returned them to the office, as any good employee would do. The payroll folks looked confused and scratched their heads while they said that they didn't understand how this could have happened. They would then take that returned check, endorse it as if they were the employee and cash it a local establishment that cashed payroll checks. The person at the check-cashing business was most likely in on it, and would take a cut of the money in exchange for not looking too closely at any identification. In the end, the scam bilked AIG for about $1,000,000 by the time the entire scope of the damage had been assessed.

All of this fleecing of shareholders didn't come without some enjoyment on the part of senior management. Holiday parties at AIG were notorious for their attendance by out-of-town invitees. Corporate America etiquette says that you should invite your out-of-town executives to things like the company Christmas party; typically, however, those out-of-towners don't come, because of the cost associated with travelling and staying, especially when you're talking about staying in New York City.

But AIG is anything but typical, and at his first AIG-sponsored Christmas party, John lost count of how many dozens of out-of-town business associates were in attendance, all on AIG's dime – the company picked up travel costs, hotel rooms, food, the whole thing. Two young ladies – Molly and Holly, who later became collectively "The Olly Girls" – were the nieces of two separate AIG executives who'd secured them jobs. John met them during a conversation he was having with Axel Freudmann; the girls immediately discerned that John was someone with connections within AIG, someone who could help to advance their "careers," such as they were. They attached themselves like remoras and held on like grim death. Not even Aimee Sharrock, John's dutiful staffer, could release their vice-like grip on her boss.

John was kind enough to introduce them to other senior level executives at the party and, after a few hours of cocktails, the girls suggested the party retire to the bar at the Ritz-Carlton, where they were staying (compliments of AIG, of course). Once there, the Olly Girls disappeared with two of the senior level executives who were in attendance, leaving John and a few others to wonder what sort of "interview" was being conducted in private.

The next morning, John received three phone calls at his office in regards to the previous night's festivities. Two were from the executives in question, regaling him with their stories of masculine conquest; the third was from Molly, who said she'd had a great time and hoped she'd see him at next year's party. Total cost to shareholders came in at about a cool million, plus the bar tab from the Ritz. Merry Christmas from your friends at AIG.

Given AIG's presence as a multinational corporation, there are plenty of American expatriates living abroad. One such group is the employees living in Hong Kong, who are given an annual "home leave" reimbursement. The idea behind home leave is that the folks who are living thousands of miles from their friends and family can go back to the States and see them once a year. AIG picked up the tab for the whole family to fly round-trip in business class. Not a bad little perk, especially when you consider that the typical tab for a family of four to fly business class can be around $30,000. So an employee might produce an itinerary that offers no advance purchase and submit it for "reimbursement," though he hasn't yet paid the fare. He gets his money – the full thirty grand – and then makes his reservation.

Oftentimes, however, the family of four would go somewhere local on a two-week vacation rather than all the way back to the USA. Thailand was a popular destination, which would typically ring in at about $5000 for the same family of four. The $25,000 they pocketed tax-free more than made up for the fact that they didn't get to see the rest of their family back home.

In the event that the person really wanted to get back to America, however, he could take his pre-paid reimbursement and buy a coach ticket, then use frequent flier miles to upgrade to business class. When you're flying back-and-forth to Hong Kong, you rack up plenty of miles to upgrade pretty quickly. Worst case scenario, if he got stuck in coach, the fact that he was paying about six- or seven-percent of his reimbursement and pocketing the rest made the whole ride just a little more comfortable.

*　　*　　*

On August 9, 2007, AIG was scheduled to have a conference call with shareholders, which is a typical occurrence. Publicly traded companies like AIG are required, in fact, to have quarterly shareholder "meetings" – oftentimes held via telephone, especially in the case of a multinational corporation with an astronomical number of individual investors – and the August 9th call was going to accommodate that requirement.

Ordinarily, these sorts of meetings involve things like earning reports, activities within divisions, who's doing what for the company, why investors should be confident in their investment, that kind of thing. On August 8, 2007, however, the day before the scheduled call, word came down from Steve Bensinger that the content of the call would be slightly modified. AIG's Chief Executive Officer Martin Sullivan said in a press release, "We continue to be very comfortable with our exposure to the U.S. residential mortgage market, both in our operations and our investment activities. However, in recognition of the significant investor interest in this topic, we will provide a presentation during our earnings call, which will be available in the investor information section of AIG's website tomorrow morning at 7:30 a.m."

The presentation in question was something of a dog-and-pony-show-cum-smoke-and-mirrors-deception. The document was a thirty-five page PowerPoint slideshow, featuring sections on all the relevant sectors of AIG's business. But before we get into the language they're using in this presentation, let's first get some terms defined. One of the biggest problems with this sort of presentation is that you, as the viewer or listener, are under the obligation to learn the language they're speaking. If you don't understand it, you're not going to get much out of the presentation.

Let's start with a CDO. A Collateralized Debt Obligation is a debt that has built-in collateral. Things like mortgages are CDOs. In investment terms, though, a single mortgage isn't that sexy, because it's really not going to net an investor that much profit. A bunch of mortgages bundled together, however, has the potential to make a lot of money as an investment product. So typically when you hear about an investment opportunity that is a CDO, it's referring to an investment product that is a bundle of mortgages or other collateralized debts. The collateral is the house itself, and the debt is the mortgage payment the homeowner owes to the bank.

The thing about a mortgage is that when you get one, you're staking your well-being to the fact that you're going to keep on making that monthly mortgage payment. If you can't make the payment and you get kicked out of your house, you're suddenly homeless. Because of that inconvenient reality, people tend to pay their mortgages first before any other bills. And if somebody does, in fact, default on their mortgage and gets kicked out, then the mortgage holder can take possession of the house and then resell it. That's why investors love CDOs. At least in theory, they're rarely going to lose money.

One facet of the American Dream is home ownership, and there are those people out there who have less-than-stellar credit ratings. As a result, they oftentimes have trouble qualifying for a mortgage. These people fall into the category of "subprime" borrowers, because they don't necessarily meet the criteria to be called "prime" borrowers.

The thing about subprime mortgages is that the interest rate is typically higher – the lender wants to offset the risk he's taking by getting paid more for his services. And that's why subprime CDOs were such a hot commodity once upon a time. When you pair together the idea that people will do whatever it takes to stay in their homes and the higher interest rate, it's a potential gold mine for investors seeking to cash in on a quick buck.

The problem with subprime mortgages is that they're very risky because the person who is taking out the loan has less ability to pay it back, at least according to his own credit history, than someone who is not classified as a subprime borrower. But investors love them, for all the same reasons that AIG thought the mortgage insurance game was going so beautifully. As I've said, people will go to the ends of the Earth in order to save the home they're living in, even people with bad credit. But people with bad credit will pay more in interest. So as a CDO investment, subprime mortgage securities offer a potentially huge return. If they get paid, that is.

But how do we get from a couple buying their first home to investors buying their mortgages? It all starts with a lender. Some mortgage lender, anywhere in the country, lends someone the money they need to buy a home. He'll take all the mortgages he writes and bundle them together into single CDO units. At this point, investment firms get involved. They buy up these CDOs in huge bunches from individual mortgage lenders, then farm them out to their own investors. So you end up with the very real possibility that an investor in Hong Kong buys a bond from an investment banker in New York City for a CDO attached to a house in Santa Fe, New Mexico. Talk about a global economy.

So let's move into the presentation itself. The second page included the following little standard bit of ass-covering business-speak: "AIG is not under any obligation (and expressly disclaims any such obligation) to update or alter its projections and other statements whether as a result of new information, future events or otherwise." In other words, when the mortgage market crumbles around them and they're at the precipice of losing $10 billion, they don't have to tell anybody. That's a big number, ten billion, especially when you write it out numerically: 10,000,000,000. As John says, "That's a lot of fucking zeroes with not a lot of heroes." But sleep easy, Mr. Shareholder. We'll tell you everything we know, unless it makes us look bad. Then we'll just keep it to ourselves, thanks to our trusty disclaimer.

Bob Lewis, the head of Risk Control for AIG, was the point person on the presentation. He detailed for anyone who cared to listen AIG's involvement in the mortgage market, and explained how AIG served in both the position of the mortgage creator – i.e. the person who lends you the money in the first place – and the position of the mortgage insurer – i.e. the person who comes to the rescue if you default on your mortgage. The conflict of interest inherent in that pairing is almost too much to fully comprehend. It's like betting on your own team when you're the coach.

Mortgage insurance is one of the most lucrative rackets going in the housing market today. If your financial means are limited and you're down payment is less than 20% of the purchase price of your home, then you're oftentimes on the hook for mortgage insurance. Mortgage insurance is just like any other kind of insurance – you pay your premium and hope like hell that you'll never have to use it. In this particular case, if you have to use it, it means you're in foreclosure and are losing your home. So in the case of mortgage insurance, you're *really* hoping you never have to use it. Regardless, mortgage insurance never pays off to actually help the homeowner. It only protects the lender in the case of default.

So the typical homebuyer scrapes together a down payment for his first home, and then he gets slapped with an extra hundred-dollars-or-so a month for mortgage insurance. He pays it because he doesn't have a choice. And if he got his mortgage through, say, American General Finance, then he's sending his money to AIG for his mortgage payments and interest. And since American General Finance works pretty closely with United Guaranty, chances are quite good that he's paying the latter his mortgage insurance premium. Of course, that's also an AIG company, so he's sending the bulk of his monthly income to AIG in one lump sum.

Bob Lewis touted AIG's track record during his time in the spotlight on that August morning, pointing out that AIG had leveraged its expertise in financial dealings to ensure that they hadn't lost their shirts in mortgage-backed securities. But that back-patting only applied to mortgages they were writing and the mortgage-backed CDOs they were investing in. It had nothing to do with the mortgages they were insuring. So while they're cheering for themselves because they were so smart in avoiding those toxic CDOs, they're also paying out massive claims to the lenders who were losing their shirts on those mortgages. In other words, as fast as the money was coming in one door, it was flying out another.

Again, it's important to remember that AIG is in the business of both writing and insuring mortgages. Oftentimes they're working in tandem; other times, however, they're only selling one or the other. So in the case of mortgage insurance, they're collecting a premium from the homeowner who is praying he'll never need that insurance. But when he does, the insurer is on the hook for a big payment to the lien holder. They had over $400 billion of insured mortgages that were carried by all the Wall Street big boys – JP Morgan, Goldman Sachs, Deutsche Bank and others. The sticky issue was that they only carried about $90 billion in cash to cover those obligations. God help them if the unthinkable actually came to pass.

But again, there's nothing to worry about Mr. Shareholder. We're in complete control. In fact, we're going to trot out some statistics and some graphs to show you just how much better off we are than the competition. And we'll throw in two little bullet points to drive home the fact that you're safe with us:

- UGC's [United Guaranty's] sophisticated default and pricing models and predictive real estate scoring systems enable UGC to manage its risk and product mix over the long term cycles of the mortgage business
- As a broad market participant in a cyclical business, UGC has experienced an average domestic mortgage loss ratio of 27% over the last 10 years

That sounds all well and good, except for a few nagging questions. For one thing, there's an overt lack of any kind of specific information. What are these models of which you speak, the ones that are so sophisticated? Or are they too far above the abilities of the common man to understand? Were they at least sophisticated enough to predict the collapse of the real estate market that everybody else in the industry saw coming? And what does a twenty-seven percent domestic mortgage loss ratio mean? Is that good? And while we're on the subject, if your predictions are that good, why isn't your loss ratio zero? One problem with this sort of meeting is that, as a participant, you're expected to listen quietly and not ask a lot of questions, nagging or otherwise.

Because they weren't kind enough to elaborate on the sophisticated models, there's not much to be illuminated there. However, in the case of the twenty-seven percent domestic mortgage loss ratio, what that means is that for every dollar that came in for mortgage insurance, only twenty-seven cents went out. So that's a profit of seventy-three cents out of every dollar they're taking in. But again, there's nothing to compare that to, so it's impossible to say how good or bad or indifferent that twenty-seven percent figure is.

Just to make sure the investors left happy, they were assured that things were headed in the right direction in terms of mortgage insurance: "Tighter underwriting standards by lenders, as well as elimination of certain risk factors by UGC, will improve credit quality of new business production. Moreover, current market conditions have reinforced the benefit of mortgage insurance, resulting in higher volume and improved pricing for UGC."

Two things jump out immediately from that, neither of them good. One is the fact that AIG is relying on mortgage lenders – who themselves are going to be selling the mortgage to an investment bank as soon as they can and thus absolve themselves of any risk – to do their due diligence on borrowers. The whole CDO market is predicated on the fact that mortgage lenders – the originators of the loans – are going to bundle the mortgages together and sell them as a package deal to an investment bank who will in turn farm them out to their own investors who are literally scattered around the world. So the guy who's writing your mortgage in Middle America, USA, may or may not care about the borrower's ability to pay the loan. He might just be more concerned with making sure he sells enough mortgages to get to go on the company cruise as one of the top performers, because once he sells that mortgage, he no longer has any stake in it at all. This is the person that AIG is relying on to make sure that their investments are actually safe.

The other major point that jumps out is the fact that they are only pointing out the short-term benefit of the dip in the housing market, namely the fact that AIG's mortgage insurance is a hot commodity because of the risk of so many people defaulting on their loans. Because the risk is so high, the premiums are going up exponentially. What they fail to say, though, is that if all of those people do, in fact, default on their loans, AIG is in some pretty hot water because they'll be on the hook for actually paying all of those mortgages that have gone south. But what are the chances of that actually happening? After all, the original lenders clearly have the best of intentions and are fully vetting all of the people they're lending to, aren't they? And people will do anything to keep their houses, so there's no real risk that it's ever going to come to AIG's having to pay out all those claims.

Unless, of course, the housing market crashes like it did.

What makes the whole thing almost funny is that the same presentation that sings the praises of the mortgage-backed securities teams also includes the fact that the AIG Financial Products division had expressly stopped writing credit default swaps (a form of investment insurance for CDO portfolios): "AIGFP stopped committing to writing 'Super Senior' protection that included sub-prime collateral in December 2005…" In other words, one group is saying how smart they were to insure these mortgages, while the other group is saying that they got out of the business of insuring them altogether because it was just too risky.

But again, the entire presentation focuses solely on what AIG is selling to the public. It never addresses the risk, the exposure, the defaults, the claims and the losses that AIG was already getting hit with from Lehman Brothers, Merrill, Goldman Sachs and the rest of Wall Street. How did Martin Sullivan, Steven Bensinger and Bob Lewis think that an entire presentation which only told the smallest part of the largest financial failure in history would go unnoticed?

Perhaps it was more willful blindness on the part of the AIG brain trust. What is more amazing, however, than the fact that they thought they could get away with it is the fact that they *did* get away with it for the most part. For the most part, there was absolutely no challenge presented to AIG by any group of shareholders on the information presented. Sullivan pulled off one of the greatest flanking maneuvers ever recorded in the history of such actions, and was paid $65 million to leave the company as his reward.

All of this good news about the mortgage insurance group flew in the face of the fact that the reports issued just the day before indicated a far less rosy picture for AIG. In fact, AIG's earnings report (as required by SEC regulations) was issued on August 8, 2007. The day before the conference call. And those earnings indicated that the mortgage insurance unit was operating at a $78 million *loss*. As in lacking seventy-eight million dollars. That compared to a $110 million gain the year prior. What happened to the life-is-good picture they painted in that presentation the next day? Where did those numbers come from? After all, we're talking about a money swing of almost $200 million. Is this what we're supposed to accept as a well-positioned business that has their fiscal practices under control in a market with a model that is working as it is designed to?

The first slide of the presentation tells you, actually: "Financial Figures are as of June 30, 2007." A full month earlier. Remember that little caveat about how they were under no obligation to update the information they were providing shareholders? At least they're being honest when they're deceiving the shareholders.

It is important to point out that using figures from the end of June for an early August presentation is not too far out of the ordinary. I don't want to suggest that AIG was somehow using specific data to support a point or make themselves look better. It just happened to fall out that way. The reason for the earlier figures is that the second quarter of AIG's fiscal year ended on May 30, and the auditors that went over those numbers — the same auditors who had been charged with policing operations like the Bermuda entity and the Panama insurance divisions — had a month to make sure that everything was right. So the numbers that the AIG folks were using were actually the latest verified numbers they had. They could, of course, have volunteered the information that things weren't quite as pleasant as they were claiming, but they chose not to.

And let's skip this idea that they got blind-sided by the collapse of the housing market. Remember that this was written — if we assume the earliest possible date of authorship — at some point in early July, right after those June financial figures they quoted came out. The later it got in the year, the more obvious the fact that the housing market was tanking. So early July 2007 is the best I can do in terms of absolving them. And by that, I mean that it's the latest date that the housing market collapse wasn't common knowledge to every man and woman on the street.

But even July is pushing it. As early as April of 2006 — more than a year before this report was compiled — financial analysts were referring to a "housing bubble." The Wall Street Journal ran an article entitled "Hot Homes

Get Cold" on April 12, 2006, in which reporter Michael Corkery said, "Home sales have been slowing for several months, but real-estate agents in some of these formerly red-hot markets have been surprised at how suddenly market conditions have deteriorated in the past few months." Corkery went on to cite plummeting sales figures as evidence of the end of the real estate boom.

What it all boils down to isn't that the guys in Financial Products or Mortgage Insurance or whatever other division were in any way less-than-intelligent. The opposite is in fact true. They were too intelligent. They thought they could get away with just about anything, because they were just that smart. And they did get away with it for a long time. In the case of the August, 2007, earnings, for example, AIG as a corporation showed a thirty-four percent increase in profit over the year before, growing to $4.28 billion for the second quarter. The Life Insurance division – John Falcetta's division – helped contribute to offsetting the mortgage insurance group's losses by turning in a $2.9 billion profit. It was the more profitable groups – the ones who were at least also turning out products that actually added revenues to the company's bottom line – that helped the Mortgage Insurance group escape the consequences of their own losses, and for AIG to continue to tell their shareholders that there was nothing to fear.

The report, released after the close of trading on the New York Stock Exchange for the day, fueled an 18-cent-per-share gain in after-hours trading. The stock price flirted with a $68 plateau. It would eventually climb up to just over $70 on October 10, 2007. Shareholders were happy. And then the truth came out. And within a year, the stock price had dropped to a previously unthinkable point below $3. If a stock price is a reflection of shareholder and consumer confidence in a company, one shudders to think what a drop of that magnitude says for the confidence people had in Martin Sullivan.

When it's all said and done, the presentation that replaced the shareholder meeting was planned to deceive. It was purposefully planned to buy time, and it succeeded in doing exactly that. John Falcetta was sure to register his complaint about what he knew to be at best a questionable move by his superiors.

In a tower of thieves, the thief who steals the most is the king. And this report, while full of potentially useful and positive information, was missing much more information than it actually provided. And none of that absent intelligence was positive news, interestingly enough. It was a tool for the thieves to cover their tracks. And like I said, the only thing more amazing than their attempt was the fact that they pulled it off with innumerable individual shareholders watching them do it.

The complaint that John filed was his own death knell. He was fired days later.

*   *   *

The laundry list of shareholder abuses goes on and on. It's not unique to AIG; shareholder abuse runs rampant in corporate America, though oftentimes it's better disguised than others. In one sense, this entire book is about corporate shareholder abuse of one type or another, because the abuse of the public's trust is equally condemned in the minds of many as the abuse of funds is. One has to marvel, though, at the complexity and daring of some of the scams that employees at all levels of the corporate food chain come up with as ways of furthering their own ends.

One of the greatest corporate boondoggles that John described, however, didn't involve a scam of any kind. It merely involved an inflated sense of one's own self-worth and the inability to think like somebody who has an ounce of fiscal responsibility in his entire makeup. A member of the AIG management team was at a conference in Paris, France. At this conference, she received a three-ring binder of documents: notes, spreadsheets, presentations, that sort of thing. It was a big binder – a couple of inches thick, even, and full of important papers and notes and doodles – and it was going to be pretty heavy to carry it from where her car service dropped her off at the airport all the way to the ticket counter inside, were she would finally be able to hand off the massive package so the ticket agent could check it for her when she left Paris for New York City.

So she went to the front desk of the hotel where she was staying to inquire about a Federal Express box that she could ship it home in. Because it had to be shipped via Fed Ex. It was a really important binder, after all, in addition to being very heavy.

The clerk at the hotel front desk was happy to oblige her. But there was one catch. She couldn't charge it to her room, which AIG was paying for. Instead, she'd have to pay the money to ship it herself, and then include that line-item on her personal expense report that she'd later be reimbursed for. But rather than just pony up the money and wait a few days to get paid back, she called her secretary in New York City (at international rates, on AIG's tab) and had her ship an empty Federal Express box with an AIG shipping label attached to it (also compliments of AIG). And because she needed it quickly, she had her send it by – is there any other way? – Federal Express.

So an empty box was shipped in another box from New York City to Paris. But the management executive was in too much of a rush to wait for the empty box, so she checked out of the hotel before her box arrived. The front desk clerk signed for it when it arrived and, knowing that it must be important because it had been shipped via Federal Express, he immediately had it sent via special courier to the AIG offices in the La Défense section of Paris, the cost of which was billed to AIG.

The receptionist at the AIG office signed for it. By the time the courier arrived there, however, the management executive – who at this point in John's description had achieved the title of "management idiot" – had left that location with her heavy three-ring binder in tow. But when the receptionist found out that the would-be recipient was no longer dans le bâtiment, the courier had already left the office to head out on yet another mission of delivering only the utmost of important packages. So she called a new courier and had the empty box delivered back to the hotel, because she had no idea what else to do with it.

When the new courier delivered the empty box back to the hotel, they told him at the front desk that they were terribly sorry but they couldn't accept it because the guest in question had left the hotel. By this point, in reality, the guest in question had left the country, toting her heavy three-ring binder all the way with her to the airport. So the courier returned once again to the AIG office, billing the firm for a round-trip fare.

The receptionist at the AIG office by now knew that this box must contain something vitally important, so she put it in yet another Federal Express box and shipped it back to the AIG Tower in New York City with the utmost of haste so that the recipient would have her important package with as little delay as possible.

So in the end, this set of boxes that was nothing more than a cardboard set of Russian nesting dolls with an AIG shipping label inside had travelled round-trip from New York to Paris, with quite a ride through the City of Lights in between. The final tab for this little mailing fiasco topped $800 all told. For a mailing label.

These are the same people to whom the American taxpayers have given over $170 billion.

*"The way to stop financial joy-riding is to arrest
the chauffeur, not the automobile."*
—Woodrow T. Wilson

CHAPTER NINE
"The Jig's Up"

As is customary in classical tragedy, you already know how this story turns out. In classical drama, it's standard protocol for the audience to know from the start how the tawdry tale is going to end. Think about *Romeo and Juliet*, for example. A lot of people think of it as a perfect tragedy – two kids fall in love, they figure out it can't work, they kill themselves. It's tragic. But consider the Prologue to the drama, the first fourteen lines of the play:

> Two households, both alike in dignity,
> In fair Verona, where we lay our scene,
> From ancient grudge break to new mutiny,
> Where civil blood makes civil hands unclean.
> From forth the fatal loins of these two foes
> A pair of star-cross'd lovers take their life;
> Whose misadventured piteous overthrows
> Do with their death bury their parents' strife.
> The fearful passage of their death-mark'd love,
> And the continuance of their parents' rage,
> Which, but their children's end, nought could remove,
> Is now the two hours' traffic of our stage;
> The which of with if you with patient ears attend
> What here shall miss, our toil shall strive to mend.

Shakespeare has just told us everything we need to know. Two kids are coming from different families that happen to be feuding. They're nice families, but they just don't get along. And it's only through the death of these two children that the parents finally figure out that life is too short to be fighting over something neither side can remember what exactly it was that they'd begun fighting about in the first place.

But first, the kids have to meet and fall in love and realize that they can't be together, or else they won't qualify as "star-cross'd." So sit back, relax and spend the next two hours watching us show you exactly how what we just told you was going to happen unfolds. That's the basic gist of the thing, anyway. Shakespeare has a gift for language that eclipses most of our abilities, and I'm certainly not claiming to be any kind of exception to that rather universal truth.

The theory behind the prologue as a dramatic device is that theatergoers in Shakespeare's times weren't privy to things like flashing lights to let them know that the play was beginning, nor did they have pre-production publicity to tell them what the story was about. So oftentimes, playwrights would kill two birds with one stone. You have a brief introductory speech that lets the audience know that the play is starting; if you miss it because you're talking to your neighbor, it's not like you've missed anything crucial, because you're going to see the prologue acted out over the course of the play. But it does let you know the play is starting. Additionally, if you're walking in totally cold and have no idea what the play is about, the prologue will let you know, in very brief form, what's about to happen.

In the case of this book, John's wife Lauren told you what happened on December 18, 2007. It was a week before Christmas. John and Lauren were at their home on Nantucket, planning for a joyous holiday. Lauren was expecting the couple's third child. And then, in the oft-overused blink-of-an-eye, those plans were thrown into absolute and utter disarray as federal agents descended on the house and took John into custody. And now you know the whole story, the back story that Lauren didn't know anything about when the agents came into her house that morning. But the story of the months between John's termination by AIG and his subsequent arrest have yet to be told, as does the story of what happened next.

In his final days at AIG, John knew the end was coming. John now feels that the first time he opened his mouth to object to the Bermuda project was the beginning of the end, but the process didn't surface overtly until August of 2007, the same time that the tax issue was getting "resolved" by trying to cover it up where it needed to be and by seeking amnesty and falling on their swords where they had to.

That year, the ALICO strategy meeting was scheduled to be held in Monaco. Monaco is many things, but a cheap destination is not one of them. Wives and girlfriends were, of course, invited and encouraged to attend as was AIG's custom with such events. And the wives and girlfriends – may they never meet – were more than happy to attend. After all, it wasn't every day that your boyfriend or husband's company offered to pay for a first-class vacation in Monaco for you.

John got a phone call from David Fravel, he of the generous house purchasing program. Fravel told John that, as a money saving move, they weren't going to be having any HR-related planning going on at the strategy session, so John wouldn't need to attend.

Knowing of Fravel's penchant for wasting AIG's money whenever the opportunity presented itself, John figured that something was up, and he asked Fravel, "Don't we need people to plan whatever strategy you all come up with? And don't we need people to execute the strategy once it's in place? It seems to me that we would, and the best way to accomplish those goals would be to have me there."

Fravel was silent on the other end.

"Look, David," he said. "If I'm not wanted there, just tell me so. But don't bullshit me here."

More silence. The conversation was clearly over. The company would be saving money on a corporate junket to Monaco that masqueraded as a meeting of the senior management team by excluding their Human Resources Vice President. It might have made sense to Fravel; John, however, didn't see the logic. In the past, whenever he'd been unable to attend a meeting, it had created a huge problem for Rod Martin, who let John hear about it.

Two days later, John received a disturbing phone call from a credit bureau that he'd contracted with to monitor his file. They informed him that AIG had pulled his personal credit file. While this wasn't necessarily an out-of-the-question kind of action on their part, it was certainly odd behavior to be exhibiting towards somebody in John's position. After all, he wasn't applying for a job. He'd already worked his way in, so they should have no reason to pull his file at this point.

That news was the second of two odd things that, taken separately, weren't really anything much. First it was his being disinvited from the annual budget meeting, and then it was the notification that his employer was taking a sudden interest in his credit file. Separately, they were benign enough in and of themselves. But taken together, they were the beginning of a pattern.

The third straw, which was the one that really started setting off sirens in John's brain, was probably also the one that, independently, would have made the smallest blip on John's radar. He called Steve Gorman to discuss an issue that Gorman had been hounding him about. Gorman had said that he couldn't resolve the issue in question without John's assistance, and he'd been hot and bothered about it for a couple of weeks. John finally had the time to devote to it, so he called Steve to tell him so. Gorman told him he didn't need the help; he'd take care of it himself. Again, not a wildly odd occurrence; it's just a senior executive doing a little work. Finally the guy was taking some initiative and getting the job done by himself. Ordinarily, they give you a plaque or an engraved glass paperweight for doing something like that.

But taking it together with the other two components that had popped up recently, John knew it was now an official pattern, what he called his "Theory of Signal Detection," something he'd developed during his days at Campbell's.

He knew it was coming, but there was one more stop on this merry-go-round of coincidences. Edmund Tse took him to lunch. The pair sat for over two hours, Tse treating Falcetta like a long-lost best friend who he'd suddenly stumbled upon quite by accident. It was so far out of character for him that John knew something was going on. Maybe they were ransacking his desk and file cabinets back at the Tower while Tse kept him occupied at lunch. Or maybe they already knew what they needed to know to send him packing and they were just getting their ducks in a row in preparation for his return from lunch, when they'd pounce on him like cats on a mouse.

And then the official end arrived, rather unceremoniously.

As John told me on more than one occasion, AIG employees had an odd habit of "retiring" early, oftentimes just before major milestones kicked in that would have allowed them access to major bonus payments; their "early retirement" negated any such bonuses, however. Alternatively, a lot were let go due to "administrative cutbacks," again, oftentimes right before a major bonus clause was set to kick in.

Regardless of what the "official" press release told the world, all of those who fell into this category that John had had contact with during his relatively brief tenure at AIG had lost their jobs because they hadn't agreed to fall in line with the party. They asked too many questions, they refused to go along with whatever latest accounting game the company was playing. In other words, they weren't "AIG team players."

And as should be crystal-clear by now, John was many things, but an

"AIG team player" was not one of them.

His outspoken refusal to participate willingly in the Bermuda payment scam and the accompanying global income tax evasion conspiracy was as good as a resignation notice, albeit a long and drawn-out one. It took two years, but somebody had finally had enough of John's resistance. And whoever that person was — or who those people were, as the case may have been — John never found out for sure. He had his ideas. And maybe somebody had caught wind of his insider self-dealings; there was no way for him to be sure.

Regardless of who the hatchetman (or men) had been, those with the authority to make those types of decisions hadn't gotten to where they were by firing people for no reason. Whenever somebody took early retirement or fell victim to downsizing, there was always a paper trail that somebody could follow in order to demonstrate the cause for letting that particular employee go. In other words, if it came back to AIG, the company was clear of any misdeeds because they'd kept meticulous records. Oftentimes that paper trail was flimsy — something of a crepe paper trail, if you will — but it was there nevertheless. In John's case, the trail wasn't really even as strong as crepe paper. At least not at the beginning.

On Monday, August 20, 2007, Steve Gorman called John in to a meeting with two AIG Internal Audit investigators. Internal Audit is the group that serves as, for lack of a better term, the police within AIG. It's their job to investigate situations that involve potential malfeasance on the part of employees and, when their findings indicate guilt on the part of the employee being investigated, to take appropriate action. Action which can, if the offense is considered to be egregious enough, go up to the point of terminating the employee for their violations. These were the same crack investigators who'd managed to remain blind to the issues presented by Bermuda, Panama and several other AIG entities that were operating in quasi-legal territory.

John found himself seated in front of a table, with the two investigators sitting across from him. The threesome sat for a few minutes in what was an increasingly uncomfortable silence. Finally the Mexican standoff was broken when one of the investigators began the interrogation in what struck John as an incredibly juvenile way. "Do you know why you're here?" he asked John, who had an immediate flashback to a trip to the principal's office in third grade. This was the part where John was supposed to be overcome with such a sense of personal guilt that he spilled his guts and admitted to everything from being the second shooter in Dallas on November 22, 1963, to the reason that the Chicago Cubs hadn't won a World Series in a hundred years, and everything else in between.

The problem was, though, that he didn't know specifically why he was there. Of course there was a litany of reasons he could catalog for the investigator if he'd really wanted to. He knew it was because he'd been outspoken about Bermuda – that was the real reason, though he knew they wouldn't publicly admit it – but he didn't know what specific offense they'd dug up to use as their excuse to get rid of him. Maybe they'd found out about his use of the 654 accounts to cover his own headhunting scheme. Maybe they'd found out about his misrepresentations on his résumé. Maybe it was something else they'd managed to dig up. There was no way of knowing, but he was about to find out from them, of that he was fairly sure.

So despite the laundry list of potential offenses they could refer to, he truly wasn't sure what they knew and what they didn't in regards to his own shady activities, so he just kept his mouth shut. He sat there trying his best to be polite, to look puzzled, to act like anything but overtly guilty. It was an act; he wasn't any of those things – with the possible exception of guilty – but it was all part of his poker player façade. Don't give your opponent any tells about what you're thinking.

"No idea," he finally managed to say with some degree of conviction. It was, at least partially, a true statement. But he had a pit in his stomach as he thought about the conversations he'd had over the past few days. Fravel, the Monaco situation, his credit report, the lunch with Tse. Suddenly it all came flooding in on his brain in a moment of painful clarity. It was over for him at AIG. It was just a matter of how they were going to do it. He later confessed to his wife that, in that moment, it was as if a mammoth weight had suddenly been lifted from off his shoulders and he felt a wave of relief wash over him with the surety of his impending firing. It was the end of his lying.

Finally the same IA investigator said, "We've got an approval for a limo here for a contractor. Somebody named Bob Campese who appears to be a builder from Nantucket. Who approved that limo?"

"I did," John replied flatly. "He's an AIG client." He left it at that. Today, John thinks he would have answered differently if he were given the chance. When news of his arrest broke, John said, Bob Campese — who had been a close family friend, or so John had thought at the time — broke off all contact with Falcetta and his family, despite his having been the beneficiary of many quasi-legal perks from AIG, compliments of John. The limo ride to and from Yankee Stadium for a Red Sox-Yankees game that the investigator was asking about was just one instance.

"He was a friend of mine once upon a time," John would later say about the general contractor. "My wife used to make his kids Easter baskets and deliver them to his house. Now I think he's just a fat slob who took off with a half-a-million of my dollars." He paused for a moment and laughed. "Good for him," he added with a conspiratorial wink. "Better him than me."

But as far as the investigators at the time were concerned, Bob Campese was an AIG client whom John had been wining and dining in the normal fashion. Easy enough. One down, but John had no way of knowing how many more "violations" there were in the hopper that he'd have to answer for before this meeting was officially adjourned and he was allowed to go back to his job. Or to leave the Tower once and for all.

"And can you explain this?" the investigator asked as he sifted some papers on the desk in front of him, pretended to read whatever it was that he was now accusing Falcetta of, looked back and forth between John and the papers and finally decided on a single sheet that he slid across the desk so that John could see what incriminating evidence they'd managed to dig up on him this time around.

John almost burst out laughing when he saw a copy of a credit card statement. His corporate VISA card. The one that his office – he himself, in fact – paid the bill on with AIG's funds. The one that was intended solely for business purposes, but of course that was one of those wink-wink things that nobody actually ever followed to the letter. If anybody knew the extent to which employees tended to abuse their credit cards by trying to justify questionable purchases, it was a Vice President of Human Resources. But of all the things John kept sacred in his business dealings, it was the financial bottom line. He was one of the few people he knew of who religiously protected his corporate credit card, using it strictly for business-related purposes. Because of his position, he saw the waste that was so prevalent in others' use of their cards. He refused to sink to that with his own card, however.

He briefly scanned the statement. There were lunches, car services and assorted other things associated with John's daily business expenses. He didn't see anything that amounted to an offense worthy of his being fired. Unless, of course, they were going to use the fact that he was overweight and perhaps ate a little too much and thereby ran up the bill higher than he should have as a reason. It was a stretch, but this was AIG, so anything was possible, he reminded himself.

He looked up from the bill and made eye contact with the Internal Audit investigator, who looked away. It was, John knew, a tell. Even the investigator thought this one was bogus, regardless of who told him what. John finally broke the silence. "Yeah, it's a copy of the bill from my company VISA. Big deal."

The investigator cleared his throat and turned the paper so he could read it. He slid his finger down, stopping at one particular entry and, without lifting the paper or his finger, twisted it back so that John could read the entry he was indicating.

The entry in question was for the purchase of music his assistant had legally downloaded from iTunes for him.

John laughed. This time he couldn't help it. "Seriously?" he asked. "My assistant downloaded some fucking music for me before I flew to Hong Kong. You know how long a flight that is? You go direct, you're talking fifteen or sixteen hours," he said. "I bought some music to listen to on my iPod. I reimbursed the company for it, just so we could avoid any conversations like this. You can find it yourself on the HR ledgers, if you'd take the time to look."

The other IA investigator in the room took this opportunity to speak up. "He's right, Mike. We have $23,000 in reimbursements from his bank account. That covers the music plus a few other things."

The investigator shot a sideways look at his partner that John interpreted as a sign for him to shut his mouth. He then looked back at John, took a deep breath and shook his head. "It's not that easy, Mr. Falcetta," he said, his voice a flat monotone. "That's just one instance. We've got multiple instances of your abuse of both company resources and company time." He went on to explain that John had violated AIG's corporate Internet use policy, which explicitly stated that no employee would be allowed to engage in personal commercial business on AIG-owned equipment. And though he didn't mention the fact that the original intent of the policy was to ensure that employees weren't running side businesses out of the office, he did inform John that purchasing and downloading music was an act of a personal and commercial nature. And he added, for good measure, that downloading music onto his laptop could also be construed as a violation of the policy that forbade employees from deliberately clogging the corporate network.

And just when John thought it truly couldn't get any more ridiculous, the investigator went on to berate him for his "theft" of company time by downloading music to his computer. If, the investigator reasoned in what struck John as a way that indicated he'd devoted way too much time to it, the average song took thirty seconds to download, then John's assistant had stolen hours of time from AIG, all at John's bequest, which made him guilty of the "crime," too. And if his salary were divided up into an hourly rate, that chunk of hours equated to quite a lot of money that he had, for all intents and purposes, stolen from the company.

The whole scene was too ridiculous for John to really grasp. Here was a little weasel of a man telling him that he'd stolen from the same company whose fraudulent actions had made his own crimes pale in comparison. The real crimes he'd committed, that is, not this downloading music nonsense. That wasn't even a crime, and for this overpaid rent-a-cop to suggest otherwise was beyond asinine.

The investigator who was in charge suddenly struck a pained expression, like he'd just bitten into a lemon. "What's more, Mr. Falcetta," he began uncomfortably, "we've got evidence that you used the Internet from your own office here to make appointments..." His voice trailed off and he cleared his throat. "With prostitutes," he finally managed to spit out.

John swallowed hard. It was true. He'd hired hookers over the Internet. But they'd been for other execs, other clients, all with plenty of unspoken blessings but, of course, still illegal. Even still, though, he was going to have to take one for the team here. At that point in his career, he was many things, but someone who ratted out fellow execs who were seeking to get in a little extracurricular activity with women that weren't their wives wasn't one of them. The title of corporate rat wouldn't come until he sat down to tell me his story for the book you're now reading. He took the rap for the hookers, apologized and sarcastically promised never to do it again.

And then came the bombshell that had, in the back of his mind, been hounding him for the duration of his time at AIG, just as it had so many times in his past. "Your Social Security number doesn't seem to match the one that appears on your payroll record. How do you explain that, Mr. Falcetta?" The question hung in the air like a bad odor, and John decided that he had no explanation, one which had always eluded him every time this moment of truth had come up in his past. He was now officially done at AIG, so to his mind, there was no point in explaining anything.

What's more, John couldn't explain it if he'd wanted to. At least not in any way that would satisfy these goons, so he just told them what they already knew. "You're absolutely correct," he said. "The two numbers don't match."

Then both investigators turned it on full steam. They started with the whos, the whats, the wheres, the whys, all the questions that John knew were coming but which he would not answer under any circumstances.

What struck him at the time, though, was that they hadn't managed to uncover his headhunting scam. At least he'd gotten away with that to this point, but he made a mental note that he might want to cool things for the time being, until everything blew over, however long that might take.

John looked at both of them individually, maintaining eye contact for a few seconds before shifting his gaze. He wanted them to know that he was not intimidated by this act, because he had his own little secret knowledge that was going to bring these idiots down with him. "Look, guys, you're doing a job here. I know that and I appreciate it," he said. "I've admitted to three separate policy violations here, you've got me on the Social Security number. Let's just get this over with. I know you're doing this because of the Bermuda issues and all that other garbage. Just slap me on the wrist so I can get back to work, okay?" He was throwing a dart in the dark, just to see if he could hit the bulls-eye and keep his job.

At that point, Steve Gorman walked in. "John," he said sternly, "why don't you take the rest of the day off."

John hadn't heard him come in. But when he heard the tone of voice Gorman used and the words he'd said, he knew instinctively that a "day off" meant "the rest of your life." He was being terminated from his position at AIG. That much he knew.

"Fine by me," John grunted. He stood and walked out, followed by Gorman. He went to his office, where he left his keys, company identification and credit card. He grabbed the framed photo of his kids that sat on his desk, along with a thick Federal Express envelope that happened to be sitting there. It was an envelope sent from Tom Pombonyo.

More invoices, no doubt, but he knew that he wouldn't be able to get these paid by AIG. It absolutely wasn't worth the risk now that he would no longer be the one approving the checks. And leaving them here, even in the garbage, could be disastrous for all of them, because he was sure that investigators were going to be sniffing around now that he wasn't there. These invoices, if anybody took the time to look closely enough, would blow Falcetta and his friends out of the water and straight into prison. He casually slid the envelope into his briefcase.

With that, he left his office for the last time, escorted by one of the

Internal Audit investigators who'd been interrogating him earlier. The pair rode down the elevator in silence. But as John stepped out on the ground floor and walked towards the front door, he turned to his escort and said, "Don't forget I know about Bermuda. You tell those fucks that. Tell them I know everything about Bermuda and I'm going to the SEC with it." Though he never made good on his promise to go to the SEC, the threat was an initial sortie of missiles that would mark the start of his own personal war.

Later that afternoon, before word had gotten around to everyone that John Falcetta was no longer employed by the Life Insurance division of American International Group, another envelope arrived via Federal Express next-day delivery. It was from Justin Broadbent. It was another batch of invoices. But John wouldn't learn of their existence until it was too late.

*   *   *

John took a cab to Brooklyn to get a haircut. There was an old barber shop there that he frequented when the need arose, and he thought that this afternoon was a pretty perfect day for a haircut. So off to Brooklyn he went. One of the great things about New York City cabs is that the back seat might as well be a confessional booth, with the confessor cordoned off by a thick plexiglass window. During the ride to Brooklyn, however, John wasn't so much in the mood to spill his soul to his driver. Rather, he turned inward. He was overcome with varying emotions, emotions that changed with every passing block. He went from intense worry about the future to an equally intense feeling of relief that he no longer had to worry about Bermuda and the headhunting schemes and all the other issues he'd gotten himself wrapped up in. By the time he arrived at the barber shop, he'd settled on contentment with the situation as it was. He'd achieved a sense of serenity in the knowledge that the entire situation was out of his hands at this point.

After getting his hair cut, he thought that a couple of slices of pepperoni pizza and a movie might just take the edge off of what had been a relatively ugly morning. Before he could get his lunch, however, his phone rang. He figured it was Gorman, but was surprised to hear the voice of Steve Tursi, Head of Global Security at AIG. Steve's voice sounded panicked.

"I'm outside your apartment, Mr. Falcetta," he said hurriedly. "I want your cell phone, your BlackBerry and your laptop. I need them all right now."

"Hi, Steve," John said. He was in control now, very relaxed, very comfortable. He sure as hell wasn't going to rush back to his apartment to give Steve all his electronics. He was going to enjoy dragging this game out for as long as he thought he could. "No can do," he said. "I'm getting my hair cut."

"Mr. Falcetta," Steve said, his voice rising in intensity, "I don't think you understand. I need those things right now."

John laughed slightly. "No you don't need them, Steve. You can pick them all up tomorrow. I'm busy right now."

"Now, Mr. Falcetta."

For a moment, John lost his patience. "Steve, go fuck yourself," he said with conviction. "I no longer work for you people. You don't have any power over what I do and when I do it. I told you I'm busy right now, so you'll have to come get them tomorrow." He hung up his phone. The anger and resentment was growing inside of him, and he knew he couldn't sit through a movie in this mood. So he made his way back to his apartment. When he got there, John saw two blue Chevrolet Impala sedans with blacked-out windows waiting outside his building. AIG had sent an army of people to retrieve a cell phone. They had apparently gotten his warning about his SEC plan and taken it seriously.

As John neared the front door of the building, Tursi stepped out of one of the sedans and approached him. John invited him to ride up with him in the elevator, but advised him that he'd have to wait outside his apartment door. Tursi wanted to come in, but John pointed out that he had no warrant so he would not be allowed in. They rode up together to John's floor, and Tursi escorted him as far as his apartment door. John entered, closing the door behind him, and retrieved his AIG-issued BlackBerry, cell phone and laptop computer. He stuffed all three into the AIG-issued black laptop bag. It was all very quick and easy. He was in a hurry to get the stuff back to Tursi and get him out of his life.

So quick was John in gathering together all of the electronics that Tursi was demanding right then and there that in his haste to get them in the bag, John managed to be so careless as to let the hard drive slip out of the laptop. He knew it was clumsy of himself – he'd accidentally pressed the button that released the hard drive, when he thought about it, in fact – but Tursi was in a hurry and John wanted to help as much as he could. So he zipped the assorted electronics, including the now-hard drive-less laptop, into the case, opened the door and handed the bag to Tursi.

Steve unzipped it – he wasn't, after all, born yesterday – to make sure everything was inside. Satisfied that it was all present and accounted for, he zipped the bag shut again.

John decided to get one last jab in. "It's fine, Steve. I already got everything I needed off that computer," he said. "Too bad they made you rush out here with all that support staff you brought with you." By then, though, Steve was down the hall and out of earshot.

The next morning, there was a knock on John's door at 6:30 in the morning. It was a DHL deliveryman with an envelope that was labeled "URGENT" and "Hand-Deliver to Addressee Only." It was from Anastasia Kelly, General Counsel at AIG. John wasn't overly shocked by the fact that

Anastasia was sending a letter; rather, it was the method with which it was delivered that had surprised him. AIG had a long-standing agreement with Federal Express to handle deliveries. He'd heard rumors around the office that when they wanted to keep something under the radar, the AIG powers would use DHL. But he'd always thought they were just rumors. Here it was though, staring him in the face as a crimson and gold envelope. They obviously knew what he had, and the letter from Anastasia confirmed that fact.

It should be noted that John found the salutation to be hysterically funny, given the fact that he'd been terminated from his position at AIG less than twelve hours earlier:

Dear John:

It has come to our attention that as early as April of 2007 and as recently as a few weeks ago {the letter was dated August 22, 2007} you downloaded correspondence, documents and data at least four times from your company computer via your personal Yahoo.com internet account...These downloads contain extensive proprietary, confidential and attorney-client/attorney work product privileged information belonging to AIG ("AIG Confidential Information"). We write to demand that you immediately return to AIG all such information, delete any copies you may have and cease and desist from distributing or otherwise disclosing or using any AIG Confidential Information.

Both the AIG Code of Conduct and the AIG Employee Handbook contain provisions obligating employees to safeguard and avoid unauthorized disclosure of AIG Confidential Information. Your obligation to abide by those provisions continues notwithstanding the termination of your employment with AIG. In particular, the AIG Code of Conduct provides:

An AIG employee may not disclose to any non-AIG employee who is not authorized to receive such information, any of AIG's confidential or proprietary information or trade secrets whether in written, electronic or verbal form.

In the event that an employee leaves AIG, he or she may not use or disclose to any non-AIG employee any of AIG's confidential or proprietary information or trade secrets whether in written, electronic or verbal form.

Similarly, the Employee Handbook that you received and signed for states:

In the course of employment, you will have access to confidential information with respect to the business or affairs of the company and its clients. You will be expected to respect and maintain the confidentiality of this information and to utilize it solely in connection with the discharge of your responsibilities. Failure to comply may be grounds for termination. In the event you leave the company, you may not remove, destroy or use such information for your benefit, or on behalf of a different employer, entity, or other organization.

AIG's assets, including those assets that had been under your control, remain AIG's property. Misappropriation of such assets, including transferring them to anyone outside of AIG or retaining them at your home, in a non-AIG e-mail account or in any other location, constitutes theft of AIG's assets and an act of fraud against AIG. Because the assets include confidential, trade secret and/or privileged information, the misuse of the assets also violates your obligations to protect the confidentiality of AIG's information pursuant to the above referenced provisions of the Code of Conduct and the Employee Handbook, in addition to your continuing common law duties to AIG.

As I am sure you can appreciate, and as you know from your own experience at AIG, we take the protection of AIG Confidential Information very seriously. Accordingly, you must immediately (i) return to us any and all AIG documents, files, data or information in any form that you possess, (ii) instruct any party to whom you have given such materials to return them to us immediately, (iii) confirm to us in writing that you have returned all such materials to us without retaining any copies and (iv) identify each third party to whom you have disclosed such materials.

It is imperative that you comply with these requests by no later than August 24, 2007. Otherwise, AIG will be forced to take legal action to protect its rights.

AIG reserves all rights and remedies.

Sincerely,
Anastasia D. Kelly

cc: Andy Kaslow
Senior Vice President and Chief Human Resources Officer

A copy of the same letter had arrived at his home in Nantucket. Sheriff Richard Brettschneider had personally hand-delivered the letter to John's home, leaving it with a house guest of John's who happened to be there at the time. Anastasia wanted to make sure John got the letter, wherever he happened to be camping out. They were deadly serious.

After he'd allowed the letter's contents and threats to percolate through his brain, he remembered the FedEx letter he'd brought home with him the day before, the one containing invoices from Pomboyno, and he immediately got on the phone to Tom. He explained what had happened, but assured Tom that he'd gotten the last batch of invoices, so there was nothing to worry about. He just wanted Tom to know that he shouldn't submit any more invoices to AIG; they'd had a good run, but all good scams come to an end and the idea is to get out just before that end comes, because the end usually means you got caught. John was afraid he'd hung on too long.

He called Gary next and had much the same conversation. Everything was going smoother than he'd hoped, right up until the moment he got Justin on the phone. When he told Justin what all had happened, Justin asked him a chilling question: "Did you get the invoices I sent you?"

John's jaw dropped and his heart stopped. He asked Justin what he was talking about, and Justin explained that he'd dropped a bunch of invoices into a Federal Express drop box late the day before; he figured they'd be arriving at the office some time that afternoon. John had thought he'd had it made when he got Tom's invoices off his desk. But he'd seen nothing from Justin. He had to tell him the truth. He hadn't gotten them. They were still in transit. This was, he knew, trouble. This was big trouble. He did his best not to let Justin know how worried he was, but he was really scared that this could bring them all down. For the first time in a long time, John Falcetta felt true fear.

A few days later, John's phone rang. It was Tom. He'd been getting calls at his "office" from people at AIG, people asking questions about corporate search services he'd been providing. Tom had given them vague explanations, enough to get them off the phone but probably not enough to keep them away for long.

After a brief strategy session with Tom, John hung up and called Justin, only to find out that two "executives from Human Resources," as they'd identified themselves, had shown up at his mother's house, flashing AIG credentials and asking to speak to Justin. They had a check for him to cover invoices he'd submitted to their office, they explained to her. Justin wasn't home at the time, fortunately enough, but she offered to take the check on his behalf. They explained how sorry they were, but they could only release it to him directly. They'd come back, they told her.

After hearing that story, John tried to reach Gary Santone, but to no avail. He left a brief message asking Gary to call him as soon as was humanly possible. He hung up and let out a deep breath. Paradoxically, everything was over and everything was just beginning at the same time.

It was just a matter of time now before the three of them were exposed. He looked at the phone sitting on its base, the small red light next to it indicating that the cordless handset was charging. "The jig's up," he said to nobody in particular. He picked up the phone and called the AIG travel desk to have them book him a ticket on the next flight to Nantucket. The USAir flight cost the company $780, but John thought he'd earned it. "In for a penny, in for seven-hundred-eighty-bucks," he later joked about the ticket. "Or in for a million or two," he added sarcastically. He briefly thought about emailing Gorman to suggest that he tighten ex-employee notification procedures with the travel department; he was, after all, still a shareholder, and financial abuses bothered him.

CHAPTER TEN
Merry Christmas

John found himself increasingly preoccupied by the threatening letter from Anastasia. It was full of pretty serious language, if nothing else. It begged the question as to what they were so afraid that he was sending himself. The rhetoric she employed in this letter was almost threatening, with words like "unacceptable" and "demand." And just in case John had skipped over those threats, she ended it with a pretty plain-language threat after she outlined the steps John would need to follow in order to prove that he had, in fact, deleted everything: "It is imperative that you comply with these requests no later than August 24, 2007. Otherwise, AIG will be forced to take legal action to protect its rights."

John didn't see it quite that way. He felt fully entitled to not comply with Anastasia's demands. He had a major smoking gun in his hand and, what's more, he had a host of legal protections afforded him by various whistleblower acts. So he eventually managed to put his concerns to rest and focus on what he knew he had to do.

Regardless of whose opinion says what about who owns what in electronic communications, the fact of the matter was that AIG realized on or about the day after they fired John that they had a potential major catastrophe on their hands. They had just fired a man who they had trusted with major secrets, embarrassing secrets, illegal secrets. Things that, were they to see the light of day, could do a lot of damage to a lot of people within the company. And what those at AIG who sought to do him legal harm didn't realize — or perhaps didn't fully appreciate — was that they had fucked with the wrong guy.

Fortunately for AIG, however, there was a Heaven-sent gift that had been dropped in their lap, though they didn't realize it at the time. The Federal Express envelope full of bogus invoices sent from Justin Broadbent which had, by this time, been delivered to the AIG Tower on Pine Street, was a gift to the executives who had been involved in the host of illegal goings-on in that building. In a sense, it was an early Christmas gift, just without the bow and fancy wrapping paper. And without John's announcing "Merry Christmas" when they opened it.

John doesn't know what day they figured it out, but his best guess is that somebody started combing his computer with pretty fine teeth a few minutes after – if not even before – his departure. And when they discovered that he'd been forwarding himself sensitive emails, they knew something big was afoot. That information, paired with an envelope stuffed with fake invoices for work that was never done, was a pretty compelling combination. And a useful combination, too. AIG was, at the time, a trusted entity with an unimpeachable reputation. If some former employee started bandying about accusations about income tax evasion and money laundering – and he had emails and other documents to back up his claims – then that reputation might be in jeopardy. But if there was some way to prove that said former employee had a history of scamming the company, suddenly we've got a whole new ballgame. And thus began AIG's campaign to smear the credibility of John Falcetta.

*　　　*　　　*

It is vital to keep in mind that John Falcetta admits his own guilt. He admits that he has been known to enjoy a good scam nearly since he emerged from the womb. He is a thief, he is a liar, he is a convicted felon. But it is equally vital to remember that John Falcetta is as hard working and dedicated an employee as any company could hope to find. As much of an overt contradiction as that seems to be, it is a reality that has been proven true time and again. Yes, he is lacking in formal education; but he is also more schooled in practical business applications than most MBAs coming out of the country's top-flight programs. But his past does make him an easy target for slander campaigns. And his fraudulent headhunting services while at AIG don't do a lot to bolster his claims of honesty; rather, they make him an easier target for slander.

After his dismissal, information was a premium commodity for John. What he had in his possession was certainly important, but what he thought would be more valuable to him was information about what was happening within the Tower. John was in contact with the office that managed foreign travel for AIG employees, as they still had his passport because of some international travel visas they'd been working to secure on his behalf.

John wanted it back, and he'd been in the process of trying to do exactly that before he'd been fired, because he knew the day was approaching. And he knew, too, that once he got fired, it would be a lot harder to get his passport back at all. He was repeatedly handed off from person to person; it reminded him of the Bermuda issue, the hot potato that nobody had wanted to be left holding. Now John himself was a hot potato. And then, after a few days of promises that somebody would get back to him and tell him when he'd be getting his passport, it was complete radio silence. Nobody took his calls. Nobody responded to his messages. Nothing. In the end, the company that AIG outsourced this type of work to handed John's passport over directly to the FBI, who eventually returned it to John.

While John was hounding AIG for the return of his passport, his lawyer was in near constant contact with different people from AIG. The specific content of those discussions is privileged under the attorney-client relationship, but the basic ideas of the talks concerned themselves with the issues pertaining to when AIG could expect John to conform to their wishes that he return any and all materials related to AIG's business practices that he had in his possession. A few weeks after his dismissal, the face-off between the two parties was at a standstill, and John's attorney called to inform him that AIG had retained the services of an attorney from an outside private firm. In other words, they weren't using their own internal counsel. That meant that they really thought they had something against him and they were loading for bear.

In the mean time, John kept getting phone calls from legitimate business contacts of his who were complaining that payments to them were getting held up by AIG. Headhunters who had done the work they'd been hired to do weren't getting paid. It soon became clear to John that they had gone over all of his books and were examining every single person that he'd done business with. They were fully aware that there was more than one individual who'd been profiting from John's headhunting scams; the question now was simply how many there were. And apparently somebody was very intent on finding out exactly that. The motto of better-safe-than-sorry was driving the actions of the HR department, and payments were being vetted very carefully to make sure the work had, in fact, been done before any monies were sent out.

A week later, John got a phone call from his former assistant, Jordan Seitz. He was a twenty-six year-old kid from Nantucket whose father Roger had acted as John's Realtor on the island. In 2007, the kid had needed a job, John had needed an assistant, it was a perfect match. Jordan had been let go for "disloyalty." John was blown away. Jordan was completely innocent of any wrongdoing – he hadn't had the first clue what John was engaged in – but John figured that AIG had been worried about the kid's potential sympathies lying with John. They were afraid, in other words, that he'd leak the information about their investigation to his former boss.

All things considered, John wasn't terribly worried about what they might find on him and his three co-conspirators. In the back of his mind there was a flicker of concern, but at the forefront was the knowledge that he held four aces — he had them dead-to-rights on the Bermuda program, money laundering and a host of other abuses of the public's trust. If they wanted to get in the mud and fight, John was ready to get down and dirty with them. But he couldn't believe that AIG would be willing to go after him, knowing how much information he'd been armed with during his tenure at ALICO. He knew too much sensitive information that could blow the lid off their schemes.

That belief sustained John through the late summer and fall of that year. As the months wore on and nothing happened, it seemed like he was going to get away with it. Both sides would admit nothing and everybody would go on with their lives, with nobody finding out either side's dirty little secrets. John had left the apartment that AIG had paid for in Brooklyn and permanently relocated out to Nantucket, where the rest of his family had been living in their home in the Tom Nevers area.

It was, in retrospect, an appropriate location for him to hole-up. Mark Madoff, son of disgraced financier Bernie Madoff, owned a summer home down the street from Falcetta. And in a six-degrees-of-separation twist, Lauren Falcetta was operating a business on Nantucket selling children's clothing; the tenant who occupied the building in Keypost Corner prior to Lauren was Wendy Valliere, who ran an interior design business called Seldom Scene Interiors. Wendy made quite the splash in decorating circles by serving as the interior decorator for a gentleman by the name of Dennis Kozlowski (also a former Nantucket summer resident). Nantucket, it seemed, had become something of a holding pen for accused white-collar criminal masterminds.

The night before the FBI showed up at his doorstep was, John recalled, a period of time when it felt like he "could feel the bad karma closing in." It was as if he had a black cloud hovering above his head the whole day: "I was in a temporal rage over every small thing," he recalled. "I was kicking the boys' toys on the floor, throwing out food. I was just pissed off and in a foul mood for no reason I could explain."

And then, in the early hours of December 18, 2007, all the bad karma closed in. There were six officers in total, three federal agents from the FBI, two Nantucket police officers and one gentleman who never said a word. John surmised he was from AIG, because, as John put it, "he seemed more corporate than cop."

The ride from John's home to the Nantucket Police Station at the corner of South Water and Broad Streets takes about fifteen minutes; it was a silent ride. John sat in the back of a black SUV, trying desperately to reconcile what was happening. He'd been told he was under arrest for a federal crime, something that had occurred in New York; beyond that, he was given no specifics about what crime he was charged with committing. Of course he had in his mind the idea that AIG had finally found enough evidence about his headhunting scam to pull the trigger on him.

As they pulled into the station downtown, John was taken from the SUV not by a federal agent, but by a local cop. This surprised him, as he was under arrest by the federal officials, not the local guys. And then it occurred to him that the photographer who'd snapped his picture that morning as he was led from his home would have had to have known to be there. It was then that John realized this whole thing had taken on the flavor of a personal vendetta rather than that of simply a man being arrested for crimes he'd committed.

*   *   *

Nantucket is a small, tight-knit community. As such, it lives up to every negative stereotype that goes along with all the good things associated with living in such a place. The weekly paper, The Inquirer and Mirror, comes out on Thursday mornings and publishes the week's criminal activities as handled in the town's district court on Monday mornings. For many a local – and many a summer tourist, for that matter – the first part of the paper they read every Thursday morning is the police report. It makes for great gossip, not to mention great virtual people watching.

The winter is an especially difficult time on Nantucket, as the days are painfully short and the temperatures typically in the twenties, with howling winds and frequent precipitation. The year-round population plunges to about ten thousand hardy souls, down from fifty-or-so-thousand in the summer. Restaurants and retail stores shutter their windows, going into a sort of financial hibernation until the following summer. It is during these short, cold days that the isolation of an island that occupies under sixty square miles in total and sits thirty miles at sea really begins to set in. And the island, despite the idyllic association so many have with it, has more than its fair share of alcoholism and drug addiction.

As a way of combating the island's drug problems, on January 13, 2007, Nantucket police officers arrested ten individuals who were later described as "mid-level street dealers" by Nantucket Detective Jerry Adams. The arrests were the culmination of a six-month investigation that had been dubbed "Operation Bluefish," an undercover narcotics-buying sting. The operation had involved several undercover officers, culling from local offerings and supplementing those individuals with others shipped in from off-island, all of whom posed as drug buyers. They would, by night, go to area nightclubs and purchase cocaine, marijuana, crack or whatever else was available. As part of their cover, many of the officers had taken day jobs that allowed them to more seamlessly blend into Nantucket society.

One recently-inducted officer — a young woman — was recruited to work on the task force despite the fact that she was already working on the island as a summer nanny. She was a local girl who knew the ins and outs of the island, and they thought she'd be a valuable addition. She approached her boss about the proposition, and was told explicitly by her male employer that under no circumstances would she be allowed to work as the nanny for the family if she accepted the job with the police. Despite that decree, she accepted the position, all the while telling her employer that she had declined the offer in favor of the lucrative nanny position that she had already accepted.

The family she was working for was the Falcetta family.

After the arrests were made public, so, too, were some of the names of the undercover narcs that had been employed in the operation. John's nanny, Veronica Orozco, fled the island in fear for her life. In a tragic addendum to her story, her brother Vaughn Peterson committed suicide soon after, with many outside observers pointing to the pressures arising from the news about his sister — "the nanny narc" — as one of the primary factors in his emotional problems. Because Vaughn was only a freshman in high school, options like fleeing the island weren't available to him; thus, he was stuck where he was, no doubt the target of hostilities from those whose sympathies didn't correspond with his sister's. An article in the Inquirer and Mirror that broke the news referred to Vaughn's having battled "personal demons" in the weeks leading up to his untimely death.

When news of the arrest of the drug dealers came to light and John learned that his own children's nanny had been one of the undercover officers buying drugs that led to the arrests, to say that he went ballistic is an understatement. Operating under the belief that the pen is mightier than the sword, John sat down and wrote a letter to the editor of the *Inquirer* and *Mirror*.

In that letter, John lambasted the local authorities for allowing an undercover officer who spent her evenings befriending potentially violent drug dealers to work as his nanny, adding that she had been employed by Falcetta without his "knowledge or consent" in regards to her moonlighting. The letter, which drips with dramatic irony when read in the context of hindsight, reads as follows:

> To the Editor:
>
> In your recent report about a local drug bust, the reporter mentions that the task force used undercover police and informants. One of those informants was my nanny. In a phone conversation with the Nantucket Police Department, Sgt. Clinger confirmed to my wife that this was indeed true. My nanny was a "sworn police officer" and involved in "Operation Bluefish."
>
> My family and I, without reservation, fully support and contribute to the efforts of local law enforcement, but we have come to ask, at what cost?
>
> The Nantucket Police Department put a sworn police officer in my home without my knowledge or consent. In fact, just the opposite, when our nanny told us about her "offer" to become a paid informant, I expressly told her that she could not be in our employ if she accepted the offer but we respected her freedom to choose. In full view of this, the NPD chose to march on, blind to the ordinary citizens' rights, and purposefully instructed our nanny to lie to us. Our family was put at risk as NPD allowed a sworn police officer to buy and sell drugs while being responsible for the care of my children. This is an outrage! To add insult to this breach of civic responsibility, the police department further went on to comment that my children were "never put in harm's way." Never put in harm's way, is the NPD smoking its own evidence?
>
> Weren't those the seized guns belonging to the alleged dealers on the cover of your paper? Aren't we led to believe that with drugs there comes violence? What could have happened to my children if the dealers found out about the "nanny narc?" The "nanny narc" has already left the island in fear for her own safety, yet my family, who was unknowingly put directly in harm's way, is left at risk for the recriminations of these drug dealers.
>
> As we speak with our friends and neighbors, they all ask, how could this have

happened? My answer is simple, either stupidity or arrogance. The Nantucket Police Department's sworn officer entered my home, slept in my house, ate my food, and drove my car around with my children in it and the NPD didn't think that there could be a problem with that? Since when were the police authorized to place officers into peoples' homes? Remember, this "narc" was a sworn police officer who accepted pay from the Nantucket payroll.

Words can't express the disappointment, the outrage and feelings of violation suffered by my wife and myself.

This is the real war on America and this citizen intends to fight for the rights of his family.

JOHN J. FALCETTA

John's outrage at the situation and his letter published in the January 25, 2007, edition of the paper were met with mixed reactions by the Nantucket public. One poster to an online discussion forum called "Yack On" wrote, "I find John Falcetta's letter to the editor in today's Inky rather interesting. Seems as though as far as the NPD is concerned, the means justifies the end, and the well being of innocents and their families be damned. Doesn't sound as though the town has heard the last of this situation. How much per hour does [the town counsel for Nantucket] charge? Since this 'soldier' of the 'war on drugs' (war on the people) was quartered in Falcetta's home, perhaps a violation of his rights according to the third and fourth amendments of the Bill of Rights could be construed." Another wrote, "It's a good thing the gentleman wrote to the paper, at least now no one will blame him (unless they don't read the paper)."

It has to be kept in mind that, when all of this was happening, nobody knew what had been going on during John's tenure at AIG or in the months since his firing. And nobody could even guess as to what the firestorm brewing would become by year's end. When that event took place – complete with local coverage by the press – there was nary a mention on the same discussion forum. It seemed that nobody had made the connection between the "nanny narc" and the AIG exec who'd been taken out of his home in handcuffs. Apparently the public had become so jaded to the wrongdoings of American businessmen that even when it was on the front page of the Nantucket newspaper, it didn't register with anyone.

According to John, however, one person made the connection. Sergeant Clinger, who's name Falcetta invoked in his letter to the editor, made the connection. And despite the months that had passed by the time John was arrested, according to Falcetta, it was obvious to him that Clinger hadn't forgotten. Nor had he forgiven.

*   *   *

The more John thought about the treatment he'd received at the hands of the Nantucket Police Department, the more he was convinced that Sergeant Thomas Clinger had not forgotten who he was or what he'd said about the police department. John was booked into the Nantucket jail, located deep inside the red-brick Nantucket Town Building. The jail, such as it is, has four separate cells, two on each side of a dark box of a room. It is used as more of a holding facility than an incarceration unit. If you're caught driving drunk or somehow being a public nuisance, they'll keep you a few hours and release you on personal recognizance; you come back on Monday for your arraignment in district court, or they'll issue a warrant for your arrest. If you're convicted of a crime, however, you're going to be sent to the Barnstable County Correctional Facility in Bourne, Massachusetts.

John was the only prisoner in custody, so he had all four cells to himself, so to speak. He was left alone for a period of time, after which Clinger entered the room and opened John's cell. Standing there outside the open door, Clinger asked him where Santone was. The way he asked the question made John think of a *Law and Order* episode. It sounded strange to have a local Nantucket cop asking the question; John smiled inside, thinking that Clinger was trying to make him think that the sergeant had some authority over the case, which was obviously not true. He didn't answer, so Clinger repeated the question.

"Go fuck yourself," was John's reply. He accented it with a grim smile. He thought it was a pretty good joke. He followed it up with what he thought was an even better one: "Why don't you go ask Vaughn Peterson, you piece of shit?"

Clinger didn't share John's amusement. According to John, Clinger took that opportunity to push John from behind, his hands still bound in cuffs, towards the concrete wall of his cell. John's face hit the wall first and, due to the fact that he had no way to stabilize himself with his hands, he caromed off the wall and fell to the concrete floor. He looked up at Clinger and said, "You can do better than that, I'm sure. You want to send me to the hospital, you'd better be ready to come with me, you fuck!" At that point, John says that Clinger took his cuffs off, shut the cell door without saying another word and left John sprawled on the floor.

Sitting alone, John began to think again about that photographer that had arrived at his home with almost perfect timing. The federal officers had taken him into custody, all the messy work was done, the scene had been secured. And then the photographer showed up. It was as if he knew exactly when he should get there in order to give the police the time they'd need to do what they needed to do. It was almost as if he'd been tipped off by somebody involved with the arrest.

To this day, John is sure that Thomas Clinger of the Nantucket Police

Department was the source of that photographer's tip. The Inquirer and Mirror would run the story – with the accompanying photographs – with the following description of the arrest: "John J. Falcetta, a former vice president of human resources at AIG, one of the world's largest insurance companies, was taken into custody without incident around 6:45 a.m. Tuesday morning by members of the Nantucket Police Department and FBI agents." The fact that local police were involved in a federal arrest led John to believe that it was largely a publicity stunt aimed at improving the department's image at his own expense.

Some time later – it was nearly impossible for him to judge how long he'd been in the cell, because he didn't have a watch – John was taken out by the federal agents. They cuffed him again, this time putting his hands in front of him, and transported Falcetta to the same black SUV that had brought him in that morning. He was seated in a rear seat next to Sergeant Clinger, with two FBI agents in the front. They were headed to Nantucket Memorial Airport. John rode in silence, his hands clasped together in a way that could have easily been mistaken for prayer.

At the airport, the same photographer was waiting, again leading John to believe that he'd been tipped off about when to expect him so that the local authorities could cash in on his demise. John was led from the car into the terminal by none other than Thomas Clinger, despite the fact that John was technically in federal custody. As they walked along, John unclasped his hands to give a thumbs-up. He announced in a very official-sounding voice that he earnestly believed that his constitutional rights had been violated by the local authorities and that he'd be back on Nantucket before the day was over.

Once they got past the camera, however, Clinger surrendered control of the prisoner to the two federal agents. According to John, Clinger took that opportunity to take his own parting shot: "Write a letter about this, asshole."

The federal agents then took John out to a waiting plane operated by local carrier Island Air; it was a nine-seat Cessna 402 that would fly the three of them to Hyannis. From there, another car would drive them to the federal courthouse in Boston where John was to be arraigned that afternoon.

The flight from Hyannis to Nantucket is a short one; it takes about fifteen minutes from take-off to landing. It's a loud trip to be sure, as the Cessna's twin propellers make a lot of noise inside the small cabin, so it can be difficult to carry on a conversation, not that the agents were necessarily John's idea of the perfect travelling companions. So John sat in his seat, still handcuffed, as the propellers droned on and on outside his small window.

There was a price to pay for everything, John knew, and he would have a price to pay for what he'd done. He found it interesting that society uses the words "price" and "pay" when it comes to doling out punishment. Even in the most basic of human lusts – the need to punish wrongdoers – we use terms derived from the financial world. His brain dredged up from some deep-seated place in his subconscious a quote from *Wall Street*, the 1987 movie that had immortalized the infamous line, "Greed is good." Sitting in the cramped cabin of the small plane, John remembered another line from that movie, one uttered by Hal Holbrook's character, Lou Mannheim: "Man looks in the abyss, there's nothing staring back at him. At that moment, man finds his character. And that is what keeps him out of the abyss."

John found himself at that exact moment that Mannheim was speaking about. He looked out the small window of the plane and all he could see was water beneath him. Endless stretches of the Atlantic Ocean were spread out in all directions around him. He was looking into the abyss. And that is when he found his true character. It was yet another moment of immense relief for him. He had found the truth about himself and he was able to finally say goodbye to his past.

He thought about his kids a lot and about his wife, about how horrible this whole thing had been and would continue to be, but especially right now when they didn't know what had happened or why. They had no idea what he'd done, as he'd worked very hard to keep them out of it. He didn't want his kids to think of him as anything but their dad, a superhero in their eyes. They were too young to understand what he'd done exactly, but he knew they were old enough to know what it meant that their father got taken out of the house in handcuffs. And their friends on Nantucket would know it, too, as would Lauren. He wanted so badly to call her, to tell her what had happened, to reassure her that everything was going to be fine. But for now, all he could do was sit and wait.

In Hyannis, he was shuttled out of the plane quickly by the federal agents who now, it seemed to John, felt better about the whole situation because they didn't have to pander to small-town politics. They whisked him through the small Hyannis airport to yet another waiting black SUV outside driven by a Massachusetts State Trooper. The drive to Boston from Hyannis can be a long one, and John quickly learned that it can be even longer when you're handcuffed and on your way to a federal arraignment. For over two hours, the men sat in silence, with the agents occasionally speaking to one another in very official-sounding language.

At one point, one of the agents called his wife on his cell phone and had a relatively domestic conversation that seemed strangely out of place in this setting. John's thoughts were still with his family. But every once in a while, he thought about these men who he would have liked to despise for what they were putting him and his boys and his wife through. But then he remembered that they were just doing their job. He'd been the one that had broken the law; these guys were just doing a job. It wasn't their fault that John had committed a crime; that responsibility fell solely on his shoulders, and

John knew that. These guys were innocent. Just doing their job. He couldn't hate them for that, no matter how hard he tried. His hatred for Nantucket Sergeant Clinger, however, remains fully intact. I hazard to guess that in twenty years, John will look kindly on the FBI agents who did what they were charged with doing. But he will inevitably continue to site all of America's ills on a man who John refers to as "a corrupt local cop."

*   *   *

John was transported to the Joseph Moakley Federal Courthouse in Boston. The building itself stands in sharp contrast to what so many see as the traditional character of Boston's architecture. Rather than a Colonial-style building with Grecian columns, the courthouse is an imposing structure of brick and glass, featuring a curved wall of windows looking out on Boston Harbor. Inside, it's not too difficult to confuse the building with an upscale art museum, as the interior features smooth granite walls, a permanent art collection and a seafood-themed restaurant called "The Daily Catch," double entendre supposedly not intended.

He was locked in a holding pen with four other men who were to share a single open toilet if the need arose. John had missed lunch, so he just sat on the metal bench that was bolted to the cinder block wall and listened to the sounds around him. People were screaming random noises. Nothing coherent, just ranting. And Spanish. There were a lot of Spanish-speaking men down in the pens, John realized, their voices mixing with boisterous laughter. This was, apparently to at least a few people, something to laugh about. John wasn't one of them.

When they finally called his name, John stood and went to the barred door of the cell. He was handcuffed and escorted to a small square room with thick glass windows. Inside, he met his attorneys, Robert Hillman and Steve Brooks. They pitched their idea for John's defense: he needed to tell everything he knew about the scam. The first one to roll is the first one to get out of doing any prison time, they told him. He would need to roll on his co-conspirators.

But John wouldn't do it. And it was more than just a sense of duty to his friends that he'd gotten into this mess, not to mention their families. He wasn't a rat, that much had been established. But he was more than willing to roll on AIG when the time came, and he figured that was a fish of a size that would be sure to keep him out of prison. For the time being, however, he just kept his mouth shut in regards to what he knew about AIG and told his lawyers that he wouldn't be giving up his co-conspirators or cooperating with the prosecutors in their cases. He was absolutely confident in his decision and there was nothing more the lawyers could do to change his mind. They left, and John was returned to the holding cell for a brief period, after which time he was transported to the facility to which the federal courthouse contracted out its prisoner-related services, the Plymouth County Correctional Facility (PCCF) in Plymouth, Massachusetts.

PCCF was a whole new world for John. Upon arriving at the facility, he was strip-searched and issued the standard green jail scrubs. As he was being led to his cell at PCCF, John was supposed to be shackled per jail regulations. But in John's case, his ankles were too thick for the shackles to go around, so he was chained six ways to Sunday and looked more like a Hollywoodized Christian about to be fed to the lions than anything else. The picture, to John's mind, was a comical one; to the minds of the prisoners who saw him, however, it was one of awe-struck respect. Anybody, they reasoned, who warranted that much chain to keep him under control was no doubt somebody they didn't want to screw with.

The gawking masses showered him with all sorts of jailhouse quips:

Happier Days

Photos Courtesy of the Falcetta Family

"Look! The feds got him more locked down than Saddam Hussein," one yelled. "He's that Atlanta killer," another surmised. One who was apparently a fan of mythical dinosaurs shouted, "He's Godzilla!"

And then came an unfortunate announcement from one cell: "He's a cop!" screamed a terrified voice. "I saw his picture in the newspaper! He's a fucking cop!" As John passed the cell of this would-be town crier, he made a mental note of the man's face. Several hours later, that same face would be slightly disfigured and missing a few teeth, as John took out his pent-up frustration on this misinformed inmate. John knew that a cop stood as much chance of surviving in a place like this — which housed everything from repeat DUI offenders to pedophiles to murderers — as the oft-cited snowball in Hell.

After the confrontation, John was released into the general population, and three inmates immediately approached him. John was initially scared that they were seeking payback for the injuries John had inflicted earlier. He scanned the crowd for a guard, but found nobody who would be any help if he were attacked. When the trio had come close enough to begin their confrontation, John noticed that they each carried something. One brought an apple, another a soda and the third a toothbrush. The three wise men of Plymouth County lockup. No words were exchanged; the three men handed over their offerings and left him alone. John learned later that this was a sign of respect in prison. He'd gained instant credibility and respect for himself.

After a hellacious night in PCCF, John was allowed a phone call, which he used to call Lauren. They spent their time reassuring each other, punctuated with periodic apologies from John and promises to explain everything when he next saw her. She assured him that she was fine, that the kids were fine, that she would work with the pretrial services woman in order to secure his release on bail as soon as possible.

The next day was taken up with what were euphemistically referred to as "bail negotiations." John found it amusing that he was being bartered for, as if he were a used car. The representative from pretrial services referred to herself as a "neutral third party," but the badge on her uniform belied the fact that her allegiance was definitely attached to those who were opposed to John's getting out of this place. She finally offered up what John thought was a reasonable bail amount and the Assistant United States Attorney who would be prosecuting the case agreed to it. Now it was just a matter of getting the money together and John would be free to leave.

Three days later, John was taken again to the federal courthouse in Boston, where he was led into court to be told exactly what was happening. The charges against him were read again out loud – this would be the first time Lauren heard exactly what it was her husband had been charged with – and his bail amount was announced. Both the prosecution and defense attorneys voiced their agreement with the amount and that was it. John was again led downstairs, where Lauren met him. She'd brought with her a Ralph Lauren shirt and a pair of Nantucket Reds, the pants sold only at Murray's Toggery on Main Street in Nantucket that were made famous by, among other sources, *The Preppy Handbook*.

The AUSA had requested that John be fitted with an electronic monitoring bracelet due to the fact that he was "an absolute flight risk." However, John – the "absolute flight risk" – was allowed to leave the courthouse without an electronic monitoring bracelet and without having actually posted his bail. So in essence, the federal authorities allowed a flight risk to leave their custody with a wallet stuffed full of cash and without any way of tracking his whereabouts. It was, John said later, "brutal government efficiency at its finest."

As Lauren and John drove back to Hyannis to catch a flight to Nantucket, John began the process of unpacking decades worth of baggage that he'd been carrying around with him and hiding from his wife. As he spoke, she was silent, trying to understand, trying to take it all in. For John, this was the emotional purging moment in his own personal tragedy, that moment Aristotle called *katharos*, or catharsis.

When they landed in Nantucket, John walked into the small airport and noticed the week's Inquirer and Mirror at the newsstand. There was his picture, front and center. He was handcuffed and giving a thumbs-up to the camera. He was now rich and famous. But that would change quickly, too. The federal government would soon freeze all of his accounts and seize his assets. So for a brief period, he was just famous. According to John, he'd only experience eight minutes of the fifteen minutes of fame he felt he was due; today he holds out hope that he'll get those remaining seven minutes one of these days. And then the hullabaloo around his arrest died down, even on tiny Nantucket Island. At that point, John was just poor and obscure.

"But not for long," he told me. "I found my true friends through all of this, two or three honest friends who stood by me. And I found my family. And maybe most important, I found myself, the real me that I'd abandoned all those years ago. And I'm all the richer for it." He then quoted George Bailey, the suicidal man who gets a chance to see what the world would be like without him in *It's a Wonderful Life*: "No man is poor who has friends."

*　　　*　　　*

On November 14, 2008, John J. Falcetta was sentenced to 51 months in prison, his time to be served at the Lewisburg Federal Prison Satellite Camp in Lewisburg, Pennsylvania. John was allowed to spend the Thanksgiving and Christmas holidays at home with his family before reporting to prison on January 5, 2009. John hired a black stretch limousine to drive him from his home to the prison. John explained to me before he went in, "If you're going to go, go big or don't go at all."

It was, to my mind, the perfect way for John to end this chapter of his life.

"*It is now life and not art that requires the willing suspension of disbelief.*"
—Lionel Trilling

CHAPTER ELEVEN
Resign or Go Commit Suicide

2008 was a bad year for the financial industry. Investment bank Bear Stearns – the fifth largest investment bank in the country at that time – collapsed and was taken over by JP Morgan in March of that year. It was an event that nobody believed could really happen, but as any former Bear employee will tell you, it happened. But of course it couldn't happen again. That is, of course, unless you ask any former Lehman Brothers employee, as that financial stalwart met the same fate as Bear in September.

And then the world held its collective breath as AIG – one of the largest employers on planet Earth – teetered on the precipice of collapse.

But on September 15, the announcement came down that the federal government would literally be seizing control of AIG by way of a loan. In exchange for lending the limping behemoth $85 billion, the government would take 79.9% ownership in the company.

The standard party line was that AIG couldn't fail – it was "too big to fail" – because if it did, God help us, we'd be seeing precipitous drops in the economy worldwide, the likes of which had never occurred in human history. We'd heard that same line at least twice before, mind you: once just before Bear collapsed and again just before Lehman went under.

Hank Paulson, then Secretary of the Treasury and architect of the AIG bailout, stipulated that then-CEO Robert Willumstad would be relieved of his duties, and his office issued a statement that said, "This loan will facilitate a process under which AIG will sell certain of its businesses in an orderly manner, with the least possible disruption to the overall economy."

That was the Fed's hope, anyway.

Timothy Geithner, the new Secretary of the Treasury appointed by President Barrack Obama, was charged with, among other things, overseeing the distribution of federal monies provided by Obama's bailout plan for the battered financial industry, the same one that had been started by Geithner's predecessor. Given what we know today about both Secretary Geithner and AIG, I think it is safe to say that this was arguably the ultimate financial case of the deaf leading the blind.

Before Geithner even took office as the Secretary of the Treasury, he was revealed to be something of a free financial spirit, to put it nicely. During his confirmation hearings in front of the United States Senate, Geithner begrudgingly acknowledged that he'd failed to pay $35,000 in self-employment taxes, a lapse he called, among other descriptors, "careless," "unintentional" and "avoidable." Ironically enough, the same words were used to describe AIG's Bermuda scheme by the firm's lawyer. Geithner went on to blame it on Turbo Tax, the computer program he'd used to self-prepare his own tax returns. Of course, the fact that the man who would be in charge of the largest federal reserve bank in the country and then the Secretary of the United States Treasury was using Turbo Tax to do his taxes rather than an accountant went by, for the most part, without notice. It echoed the same sort of irony from AIG's mortgage-backed securities presentation in that the only thing more asinine than the fact that Geithner suggested Turbo Tax as an excuse was the fact that so many people bought it as a rational explanation.

His excuse – implausible as it might have been – made for a nice story in front of the Senate, but consider the actual truth of the matter. The tax issue arose from Geithner's employment at the International Monetary Fund (IMF) in Washington, D.C. Non-American citizens working at the IMF are exempt from having to pay U.S. income taxes on their salaries so, as a way of leveling the economic playing field for all its employees, the IMF reimburses its American employees for their payroll taxes; however, it's important to remember that the IMF doesn't withhold payroll taxes, either, so its employees have to pay the aforementioned self-employment tax.

So for a period of four years – from 2001-2004 – Mr. Geithner filed an income tax return which presumably included his self-employment tax. And he got reimbursed by the IMF, per that organization's policy, for those self-employment taxes. The only catch was that he never paid the taxes for which he was being reimbursed. In other words, Geithner was double-dipping; he was getting paid back for money he'd never paid out in the first place and was thus doubly rewarded for his efforts. That's something a lot of people like to call "fraud" when they're throwing legal terms around in polite conversation.

Either way, it's nice work if you can get it.

And yes, Mr. Geithner has since paid all back taxes that he owed and he is to be forgiven for his transgressions. But one has to wonder if he would have done so willingly had he not been nominated for the position for which he was. After all, his conscience wasn't so battered that he felt compelled to make restitution while serving as Chairman of the New York Federal Reserve Bank. And what's more, one has to wonder about what other "oversights" he might have made. One oversight that came to light – again, only after Mr. Geithner was grilled incessantly on the subject – was the now-infamous AIG bonus scandal that rocked the news headlines in early 2009.

By March of 2009, the reality had set in that the members of the executive branches of the AIG corporate tree were not necessarily to be trusted with money, especially large sums of it. The hard truth came to light when it was discovered that, despite accepting over $170 billion of taxpayer-funded bailout money over the course of several months, AIG had paid its employees hundreds of millions of dollars in bonus payments.

The word "bonus" is defined in part as "a sum of money granted or given to an employee, a returned soldier, etc., in addition to regular pay, usually in appreciation for work done, length of service, accumulated favors, etc." In everyday vernacular, a "bonus" is a reward for a job well done. Apparently AIG's definition was somewhat different. Approximately $450 million of the firm's 2008 bonuses –bonuses that were financed with US taxpayer money — were paid out to employees of the Financial Products division, a total of approximately 400 people. Those bonus payments were even more troubling when considered in light of the fact that the company as a whole lost approximately $40.5 billion in 2008, approximately $10 billion of which was directly linked to the Financial Products division's bets on Credit Default Swaps (CDS). At the risk of splitting hairs, if $10 billion in losses merits $450 million in bonus payments, I shudder to think what employees would get if the division somehow managed to turn a profit.

Credit Default Swaps are something that, unless one is a financial guru, are typically relegated to the land of mysterious investing concepts better left to those in the financial world. And truth be told, the financial guys like it that way. If they're the only ones who really understand what they're doing, then nobody can tell them they're doing it wrong or taking unnecessary risks. A CDS is basically an insurance policy, and if any firm anywhere can attest to the lucrative nature of the insurance business, it's AIG. A CDS insures the creditworthiness of a loan – something like a mortgage, for example – by guaranteeing to pay the par value (or the value without interest) of the loan in the event of default. A CDS doesn't come cheap, and the riskier the loan, the higher the premium paid for the CDS.

So as an investment banker, if you've got a stack of mortgage bonds that you're holding on to that you'd like to farm out, you might find that you have some investors who are worried about buying them because of the risk of default. But you could assuage all of those fears if you could guarantee the return through some kind of financial insurance. Luckily for you, that's exactly what a CDS is. Investment banks would buy these credit default swaps to guarantee that their investors wouldn't lose their shirts in the event that their CDO portfolios collapsed.

In the end, the risk is transferred to the insurer, just as it is for homeowner's insurance or auto insurance. Or the mortgage insurance that AIG was touting in their presentation to shareholders in 2007. CDOs – especially CDOs that were subprime mortgages – were very popular with the CDS folks, because there's nothing to help you sleep at night like the knowledge that your risky debt is guaranteed by a third party. A third party like the AIG Financial Products division. So the lenders got their money that was supported by the collateral of a house and guaranteed with a CDS, the CDS providers got their premiums, the guy with the poor credit rating got to live in his own house. And everybody lived happily ever after. Until 2007 came along, anyway.

By June of 2007 – long after the Wall Street Journal "broke" the story in 2005 – there was the beginning of a hiccup in the housing market that was noticeable to even the average guy on the street. Prices that had been steadily rising for over a decade had begun to taper off and, in many instances, had actually begun to go down. All of a sudden, those CDOs didn't look so attractive any more. Of course, nobody was really worried, because mortgage holders were still paying their mortgages, and even if they stopped, there were those Credit Default Swaps that would come in and save the CDO portfolios. The wheels really started to come off when two hedge funds run by then-still-in-business Bear Stearns collapsed, bringing to the immediate attention of the American public the fact that the subprime mortgage situation was rapidly becoming a financial crisis. But things like Credit Default Swaps were still shrouded in mystery, so nobody thought to ask why these CDO-laden portfolios hadn't been insured.

By the beginning of 2008, the situation had become increasingly dire, and the term "subprime mortgage" had become part of the American lexicon. The term was given the same reverence as "piece of shit" to many investors, and those in finance began referring with increasing frequency to "toxic waste" on balance sheets. The housing market had tanked and was continuing its downward trajectory, and the American economy was following suit, which was in turn leading the global economy into a massive recession. And as I mentioned a moment ago, Bear Stearns and Lehman Brothers both collapsed soon after. And at about that time, as I was writing furiously to meet my deadline on the book on the collapse of Bear Stearns, I first met John Falcetta.

And then came the bailout money at the end of 2008, followed by the public outrage at the payment of bonuses in 2009. President Barrack Obama referred to the company as "reckless" and "greedy." He went on, asking rhetorically, "How do they justify this outrage to the taxpayers who are keeping the company afloat?" The anger grew to palpable levels, climaxing with Senator Charles Grassley, a Republican from Iowa, suggesting that the executives from the firm "come before the American people and take that deep bow and say, 'I'm sorry,' and then either do one of two things: resign or go commit suicide."

The new government-appointed CEO, Edward Liddy, responded to the attacks by pointing out that AIG had contractual obligations to pay these bonuses (despite the fact that he also called the bonuses themselves "distasteful"), which points out a step in this whole process that has been widely overlooked. Given the fact that the two Bear Stearns hedge funds collapsed in June of 2007 (two of the first public executions of funds laden with subprime CDOs, many of which had been purchased in 2005 and 2006), it's safe to say that the subprime mortgage crisis – and the incredible risk associated with all the CDO portfolios and CDS contracts that went with it – was pretty common knowledge, at least in financial circles. And if it wasn't, it's certainly a sure bet to say it *should* have been common knowledge. Especially if those who should possess that knowledge were expecting their bonuses for their demonstration of such exemplary business acumen.

So it seems odd, at best, that the powers-that-be within the Financial Products division (referred to as AIG-FP in contractual lingo) – the group at AIG most wholly responsible for the Credit Default Swap contracts that were the source of over $10 billion in losses for 2008 alone – chose to rewrite their bonus contract some time before the end of 2007.

As it turns out, at the end of 2006, the AIG Board of Directors and then-CEO Willumstad announced a formalized incentive bonus scheme for the top 1000 executives. The plan was to cover the compensation period for 2007. The basic idea of the plan was that all divisions within AIG would be paid bonuses based on corporate performance, coupled with divisional and individual financial goals and personal performance. In other words, the better you did, the better your bonus. It actually made sense in that regard. There were to be no contracts covering bonus payments. Each division would write its own divisional goals; John Falcetta was put in charge of managing the writing of the Life Insurance division's goals.

John drafted goals for Tse and Martin after working on the language for months. He held meetings globally, with conference calls at hours most of us would consider inhuman. But as was John's nature, he didn't see a 3 AM conference call as anything out of the ordinary when there was work to be done. He battled more than once with Jackie Aguanno to get the bonus percentages up higher for people like Fravel, Rix and Zampella. His team was led by John Lee, a bright Asian man with amazing credentials, and Aimee Sharrock, a type-A firebrand out of Merrill and Deutsche Bank. They gave John their all, and Edmund's division completed all of their bonus planning worldwide first, on-time and completely. Today, as John looks back on it, he feels most ashamed for those who trusted him. He stole from them, all the while asking them to be loyal and to trust Edmund and Rod.

All of the divisions across AIG came together with their unified bonus plans. All of the divisions, that is, except for one. Connie Miller, who was Head of Global Human Resources of AIG Investments, announced that the group she headed up – namely the Financial Products division – wouldn't be participating in this exercise and they would instead be writing their own plan that would be completely separate from the general AIG scheme. The group went so far as to write their own specific contract that covered their bonuses for 2008, a contract which was headed:

AIG FINANCIAL PRODUCTS CORP.
2008 EMPLOYEE RETENTION PLAN
Effective December 1, 2007

The timing is interesting. Remember that these are the people who supposedly know all there is to know about financial products, things like CDOs and CDSs. So they should also know that things like CDOs and CDSs are incredibly risky and will be losing a lot of money in the coming months. Perhaps they knew those facts all too well, because they wrote themselves a doozie of a contract which was effective on the first day of the Compensation Year for 2008 (which ran from December 1, 2007 – November 30, 2008). And which also began well after the market for CDO-related investments had plummeted.

Though the contract itself stretches to sixteen agonizing pages of legal and business jargon, there are a few points that make for interesting reading. Let's start with the introduction: "This document sets forth the terms of the AIG Financial Products Corp. 2008 Employee Retention Plan, effective

December 1, 2007 (the "Plan"). The Plan sets out the 2008 and 2009 Guaranteed Retention Awards to be provided hereunder to certain employees and consultants of AIG-FP (which term includes subsidiaries)." Just so we're clear from the outset, understand that this contract is only applicable to the Financial Products division folks. That's a few bodies north of 350. In a company with over 100,000 employees. In other words, these people took sixteen pages to make sure that fewer than .3% of the AIG employees were properly rewarded.

The document then goes on to explain its *raison d'être*, which includes an attempt "To recognize the uncertainty that the unrealized market valuation losses in AIGFP's super senior credit derivative and originally-rated AAA cash CDO portfolios have created for AIG-FP's employees and consultants." In other words, it's not their fault. They bet the wrong horse and, though they could have changed mid-race, they chose not to, so now they're looking at massive losses, which they were supposed to be smart enough to avoid in the first place.

But it's still not their fault. After all, according to their own presentation, they supposedly stopped writing these things two years prior. Remember when they told us how smart they were to know that this was all going to come crashing down so they said, "AIGFP stopped committing to writing 'Super Senior' protection that included sub-prime collateral in December 2005..." That's two years earlier. So either they were misleading their investors in that presentation or they're misleading their bonus providers now. They can't have it both ways, no matter how hard they try. Come to think of it, if it's guaranteed by a contract, maybe they *can* have it both ways.

But then we as readers are assured that the contract we're about to wade through is also designed "To ensure that AIG-FP's and its employees' and consultants' interests continue to be aligned with those of AIG and AIG's shareholders." Now I feel better. They're looking out for their shareholders' interests, too. And we've seen how much the AIG collective seems to value the shareholders. And what's more, the FP guys would surely hate to be responsible for driving the share price into the ground.

And then we get the *pièce de résistance*, the final goal of the document, which is "To show the support by AIG of the on-going business of AIG-FP by implementing a meaningful employee retention plan." If you really love us, you'll give us our bonuses and guarantee that we'll get them. No matter what. Because you love us. And that's what you do for someone you love. The tone to this point could be easily confused with a spoiled child who expects to get everything he wants, simply because he'll keep on complaining until he does.

That is followed by a list of definitions — twenty-nine separate terms are defined — that reads like a dictionary. There are a few choice definitions, however, that give the close reader pause. The first comes in Section 1.12, "Compensation Year." The fiscal year for AIG, as I've said, runs from December 1 – November 30. That much is laid out in this section. However, this section points out that the "first Compensation Year under this Plan shall be the Compensation Year beginning on December 1, 2007 and ending on November 30, 2008." That covers the bonuses that were paid, the ones that caused so much hullabaloo.

Did anybody catch that word "first" in the previous paragraph?

That's right. We're going to get to go through this whole rigmarole all over again, probably in January of 2010. Because, if one keeps reading in that same section, one discovers that "the second Compensation Year under this Plan shall be the Compensation Year beginning on December 1, 2008 and ending on November 30, 2009." In other words, these guys guaranteed themselves a SECOND bonus for the FOLLOWING year. Talk about forward-thinking. Of course, none of that was talked about during the uproar arising from the first time we went through this bonus payment mess.

And just to verify that, look back at the introduction. It says that the plan set forth in this contract "sets out the 2008 *and 2009* Guaranteed Retention Awards to be provided hereunder..." (emphasis mine). You can be forgiven if you missed it the first time through. The fact of the matter is that, because the fiscal year resets in December, those bonuses don't get paid typically until after the ball has dropped in Times Square. In other words, the first bonus payment – the one that caused all the commotion – wasn't paid until 2009, but it covered 2008. That means that 2009's bonus payment will get paid in 2010, unless somebody with a rational mind decides to step in and take a stand. And you want to know something funny? Both the 2008 and 2009 bonus payments are based on 2007's pay package, which means they're using one of the most lucrative years in the division's existence as their baseline amount for future bonuses. And the hits just keep coming in this thing.

Section 1.14 is another interesting definition, namely the "Covered Persons" that are detailed therein. Remember that this is a bonus contract for the Financial Products division, so just under 400 individuals. Not so fast. According to the contract, those included as bonus recipients "shall mean all employees and certain designated consultants of AIG-FP." Who qualifies as a "designated consultant?" It's interesting that a contract that goes so far as to define the group that is writing it – Section 1.03 reads, "'AIG-FP' shall mean AIG Financial Products Corp" – doesn't see the need to define a "designated consultant." What that means, at least from a cynical perspective, is that they can give bonuses to anybody who's associated with them, regardless of the work they did or the quality of that work. And regardless of who they are or who they're related to. But more on that in a few minutes.

Section 1.26 is a head-scratcher. It reads, "'SIP' shall mean the AIG Financial Products Corp. 2007 Special Incentive Plan, dated January 20, 2008, as it may be amended in the future." Doesn't sound too Earth-shattering, I realize, but there's a back-to-the-future kind of thing going on here. How does a contract that, by its own admission, is effective December 1, 2007, know what's going to happen in January of the following year? I know these guys are brilliant, but can they really see into the future such that they know there's going to be a document that will be dated at least two months after they're writing the current document? It almost sounds like back-dating of documents, or at the very least doing some kind of creative planning in order to refer to these things several months before they're scheduled to exist.

The real meat of the contract's nuts-and-bolts, however, is further in, buried under those pages of definitions and rules about who is eligible and who isn't.

The interesting reading really kicks in when we get to Section 3.02(a): "General Rule for Bonus Pool Determination. Under the existing arrangement between AIG, AIG-FP, and its employees, Distributable Income of AIG-FP is payable each year on the basis of 70% to AIG and 30% to AIG-FP employees (and consultants) as bonuses (such 30% referred to hereunder as the 'Bonus Pool'). The Bonus Pool will continue to equal 30% of Distributable Income of AIG-FP subject to calculation consistent with past practices and the provisions of Sections 3.02(b) and 3.02(c)." Simply put, the folks in Financial Products are pocketing 30% of what they make for the company, with 70% going to AIG.

We move on to Section 3.06(a): "Effect of Mark-to-Market Losses on the Bonus Pool. The Bonus Pool for any Compensation Year beginning with the 2008 Compensation Year will not be affected by the incurrence of any mark-to-market losses (or gains) or impairment charges (or reversals thereof) arising from (i) the CDO Portfolio or (ii) super senior credit derivative transactions that are not part of the CDO Portfolio."

Hit the brakes. That's a show-stopper right there.

In layman's terms, the Financial Products division gang had written themselves the equivalent of fire insurance while their house was engulfed in flames. Mark-to-market losses are those losses incurred in a position at the end of the year. So if your position in XYZ investment is $10 when you buy it at the beginning of the year and it goes to $5 at the end of the year, by incorporating mark-to-market accounting principles, you start the new year at $5, and your mark-to-market loss is $5. So in the next year, when that investment's value drops to $3, you only show a loss of $2 for that year. Mark-to-market is something like a clean slate for starting a new year.

But in the real world, where investors actually spend their own money, a decline in an investment's value is cumulative. So if an investor buys a stock – let's look at AIG, since we're on the subject – at $72 a share in January of 2007 and holds it through the year, watching it drop to $60 by the end of the year, he's lost $12 a share. But since he's starting a new year, if he's employing mark-to-market accounting, he gets to reset the price to $60 as the starting point. So if he continues to hold it and the stock drops to $2 a share, he's only lost $58 (in mark-to-market). In reality, though, he's lost the full $70 per share, because he loses the difference between the original price ($72) and the final price ($2), not the mark-to-market price ($60).

But at least the guys in Financial Products make their bonuses. And the reason they made those bonuses was because they were unaffected by the fact that their investments lost approximately $10 billion in total, a fact that directly influenced the precipitous drop in the stock price cited above. And the losses don't matter, because their contract says they don't count. Again, these people were supposed to have the financial intelligence to be able to predict market trends. At the very least, they should have been able to tell that the real estate market had already gone down the toilet.

We've talked about the 2005 article in the *Wall Street Journal*. That was followed up by a May 5, 2006, issue of *Fortune* magazine, which ran an article that said, "The great housing bubble has finally started to deflate ... In many once-sizzling markets around the country, accounts of dropping list prices have replaced tales of waiting lists for unbuilt condos and bidding wars over hum-drum three-bedroom colonials." So there's no excuse for not knowing what was happening. Let the finger-pointing begin. Just so long as you don't point at the guys that wrote the after-the-fact contract that ensured their bonuses, compli-ments of the United States taxpayers. After all, they were looking out for their shareholders.

How can a group who prides itself on its ability to work with such fab-ulously complex issues fail to see the signals? Nationwide mortgage defaults were rampant, as were home foreclosures. Banks and hedge funds were collapsing around them. A global recession was tightening its grip on the world economy. But this gang missed all of that?

And though there is the issue of that August 9, 2007, presentation in which AIG-FP was declared to have stopped selling Credit Default Swaps for subprime mortgages, there were plenty of outstanding CDSs that they'd already written floating around in the pipeline. By their own admission in that same presentation, in fact, they acknowledged that they had approximately $19.4 billion (which was the total value of 58 deals) that consisted of exposure to "deals where the underlying collateral is predominately BBB." What that means is that they had a lot of money committed to loans that weren't deemed very credit-worthy (read "subprime"); of that money, $8.8 billion was sub-prime exposure. If those investments had paid off like the FP brains had gam-bled they would, we wouldn't be talking about them right now. But as is all too familiar to all too many of us today, they didn't pay off.

It's safe to surmise that when this plan was created, the authors of it knew that the market values of the portfolio were tanked and, as a result, they wouldn't make any money. So they basically sat there and said, "Those losses don't really count." At least that's what Turbo Tax told them.

In the August, 2009, edition of *Vanity Fair*, Michael Lewis, author of *Liar's Poker*, penned a piece on the AIG Financial Products division, one which relied heavily on anonymous quips from traders themselves who had wrought the destruction and who had subsequently accepted the massive bonus payments they felt they were due. In the article, Lewis mentions a conversation with one Financial Products trader, of whom Lewis says, "He just wanted to know why the public perception of what had happened inside his unit, and the larger company, was so different from the private perception of the people inside it, who actually knew what had happened."

The answer, it turns out, is that the FP folks wanted to point fingers in a lot of different directions and come up with a laundry list of excuses – their boss was incompetent, it wasn't really their fault, they lost plenty of their own money, their boss called them all sorts of ugly names, the list goes on – for why they deserved their bonuses. None of them, interestingly enough, mentioned the contract they'd collectively rewritten that would guarantee those bonuses.

One might think, regardless of any inter-company contracts, that the President of the United States, who was actually giving AIG the money in the first place, would have the authority to tell them that they couldn't spend it on things like bonuses to employees who lost billions of dollars over the previous year. One might think – and one would be right to think – that Obama had actually made that provision a part of the stimulus package's conditions. Geithner and company, however, explicitly requested that pre-committed bonuses – like those demanded by the AIG Financial Products division – be exempted from that condition. Geithner admitted to writing that little chestnut into the stimulus several weeks after the uproar ensued.

And then came Senator Christopher Dodd, a Democratic senator from Connecticut, who was morally outraged by the fact that AIG had paid these bonuses using taxpayer money. Given that Dodd was the Chairman of the Senate Banking Committee, his moral outrage and sense of injustice on behalf of the American taxpayers arising from this inexcusable abuse of the public's trust sent a strong message, especially given that the AIG Financial Products called Wilton, Connecticut, its home base.

And then came the rumors. They were only rumors at first, but a few theories began to float around, theories that placed a little more blame on Dodd for this whole bonus mess than one might have at first thought he deserved. The rumors said that Dodd was actually aware of the fact that the bailout included language that would allow AIG to use the money for bonuses. The rumors went so far as to suggest that not only was Mr. Dodd aware, he'd also been the one who wrote the language into the bailout plan in the first place.

Dodd immediately went on CNN – the station that is all things political – and declared his own innocence. On March 17, 2009, Chris Dodd went before the American people and proclaimed that he'd had no idea that this language was in the bailout, and that he certainly hadn't had anything to do with putting it in there. He was astonished that anyone could possibly think he'd had anything to do with it.

But there's a funny thing about rumors. Sometimes some rumors have a little kernel of truth buried in there somewhere. In the case of the Dodd rumor, however, the little kernel was something more akin to an entire ear of corn.

On Wednesday, March 18 – the very next day, in fact – Dodd went back on CNN. This time he wasn't so much interested in denying his knowledge of the language. Apparently over the course of the previous twenty-four hours, he'd recalled something, kind of like a dream you remember after someone says something that reminds you of it. Dodd's appearance on the 18th was more of a public admission of guilt than a proclamation of innocence. He announced that not only was he aware of the language's existence, he was now taking full responsibility for including that language. In other words, the rumors were true.

In the space of twenty-four hours, he'd gone from flat-out denial to full-on admission. He was quick to point his own fingers, however, as he blamed the Obama administration for the whole mess. He claimed that AIG might have sued the federal government if they hadn't been able to pay their bonuses. After all, they were contractually obligated to pay them, right? And oh, by the way, as long as we're on the subject, his wife used to work for AIG, but that had nothing to do with his reasoning for why he made sure to include the bonus language in the bailout. Of course there's no conflict of interest here. Nothing to see, move along, thanks for coming.

As Arnold Drummond might have said back during his days on *Diff'rent Strokes*, "What you talkin' 'bout, Willis?"

As more and more news came to light, Senator Dodd's story got more and more holes punched in it. While it wasn't a sudden admission by someone claiming to have been on the grassy knoll in Dallas, it did seem a little shady that the gentleman from Connecticut's wife had served as an "outside director" of IPC Holdings, Ltd, a Bermuda-based holding company (yep, the same Bermuda) that was under the control of none other than AIG. And that's not to suggest that Jackie Dodd received any bonus money from AIG. However, it does point to the fact that the Dodd family was a little tighter with AIG than the senator might have allowed at first.

In fact, over the course of Mr. Dodd's political career – which has spanned five consecutive terms, beginning with his election to the Senate in 1980 – the good senator from Connecticut has been known to accept a dollar or two from AIG. Since 1989, Mr. Dodd has received a reported $281,038 in financial contributions from AIG. Again, no smoking gun here, but the barrel is certainly warm enough to warrant a second look.

And thus, in what is perhaps the most fitting way to end this chapter of AIG's history, we are faced with a situation in which United States taxpayers financed a bailout plan that was authored in part by a man who has accepted over a quarter of a million dollars from the company and who first claimed to have no knowledge of what the bailout itself said, but who later admitted that he actually wrote it himself, and whose spouse was receiving financial compensation from AIG, yet who somehow found that that relationship didn't qualify as a conflict of interest, so he allowed the bailout money to be managed by a man who failed to pay income taxes until he got caught red-handed and who was himself directing money to a company populated by executives that had committed more global tax fraud in the space of a few years than the average accountant sees in a lifetime.

It's been said before, and it bears repeating: You just can't make this shit up.

CHAPTER TWELVE
Brave New World

"O, wonder!
How many goodly creatures are there here!
How beauteous mankind is! O brave new world
That has such people in't!"
—The Tempest, V, 5. 181-183

And so we have come full circle, closing with a reference to the same English playwright with which we began this story. The metaphor of a circle – and a full one, at that – is more appropriate than a cursory glance would suggest in this instance.

Many of Shakespeare's plays – and those of his contemporaries – subscribe to the theme of the Wheel of Fortune. Not the game show that made Vanna White a household name, but rather the mythical idea that the fates controlling all of humankind operated with something akin to a roulette wheel, the top of which was happiness and the bottom of which was misery. Stories like *The Tempest* that ended at the top of the wheel in which everything ends well for the characters involved are considered comedies; those where the ending is not quite so happy – stories like *Julius Caesar* – are considered tragedies. One tenet of the Wheel of Fortune is that it is constantly in motion, bringing those too happy back down to a less euphoric state, while also raising those at the nadir back up to a level of happiness. And this turning was inevitable, regardless of where on the wheel one found oneself. The turning would continue and the process would go on, taking a person from happiness and fortune to despair and misery, with lots of intermediary stops in between those two extremes.

The process is something that bears a brief mention. The tragedy itself is a story encapsulated within its own framework – oftentimes a five-act play, for example – that offers those who experience it the chance to watch the action build to a climax, then fall off to a purging of emotions in the end. And all of this action is centered around a single main character, the tragic hero, someone who finds himself suffering a great downfall – a reversal of fortune – that comes about as a result of his own actions. The tragic hero is typically yoked with a tragic flaw of some sort; oftentimes the tragic flaw is as simple as his own pride that forces him to commit whatever act brings on his demise. And finally, once the hero has endured his tragic fall from grace that resulted from his own actions, the audience is left with a feeling of fear that they, too, could have been in the same position as the tragic hero; there but for the grace of God go they, so to speak.

The story of John Falcetta has followed, up to this point in his life, a cycle that is inextricably linked to the Wheel of Fortune, and his story is a tragedy. He is a tragic hero that brought on his own downfall as a result of his own actions, much as his wife Lauren wrote in the foreword to this work. He began at the top of the Wheel, where happiness was the ruling emotion. He had everything he could have wanted, at least to most rational minds, and ensuring that he stayed in that happy space was merely a matter of his doing his job and maintaining his status quo.

As we have seen, however, he chose a different path. He got greedy and he got caught. Perhaps it was an inevitable course of action, given the incessant turning of the great Wheel. Or perhaps it was just his own stubborn pride. Or perhaps it was something else completely, some addiction John suffered from that led him to do what he did. Regardless of the reasoning, he did what he did. And as a result, he was taken from his wife and children and sentenced to prison in order for him to serve out his well-deserved punishment. If we ended this story there, it would be a tragedy, at least in terms of the literary definition.

But the Wheel keeps spinning, and where it's going to stop is anybody's guess.

*   *   *

Alduous Huxley, the author of *Brave New World*, once said, "Experience is not what happens to you. It is what you do with what happens to you." The tragedy of John Falcetta's life would be a doubly-compounded one if he chose to sulk through the rest of his life and complain about the unfairness of his whole situation. The world would have truly been a lesser place if we had been subjected to a John Falcetta-less future. We are fortunate that he has chosen to follow a different path, a path of personal redemption.

In prison, John fell into his daily routine with relative ease. He wrote letters to the point that his output rivaled that of Elizabeth Barrett Browning, signing each one with a countdown of the remaining time he had to spend before his sentence was through. He has earned professional certifications in emergency management from FEMA. He continues to learn Arabic and Mandarin Chinese. He volunteered for a job teaching a GED class to inmates who had never graduated from high school. This last was a source of comic relief to him, as he told me once, "Who'd have ever thought they'd let me teach impressionable minds?" He punctuated the rhetorical question with a full-blown belly laugh. That's John Falcetta. A guy who can laugh at himself because he's teaching felons – a group he can jokingly refer to as impression-able minds – about the quadratic equation.

Perhaps the biggest change I saw in John from the time I first met him to today is a new sense of humility that has come over him. Humility is a far cry from humiliation, though the two words share a similar root. Humility is that elusive quality so many of us strive for, yet so few of us actually find. It's that characteristic that is the absolute paradigmatic opposite of haughtiness. The joke about humility is that once you think you've got it, you don't.

And John's got it. He won't admit it – that would, after all, mean he'd lost it – but it's there. Gone is the swagger, the don't-fuck-with-John-Falcetta bravado that once seemed to emanate from his every pore. Today, John is much more introspective; he's much more in tune with what is important in the world. And he's grown to understand that there are things more important to him than money, a fact evidenced by his current salary as a federal inmate. In exchange for teaching the GED class, John is paid the princely sum of nine cents an hour. And today he's grateful for that income. What was perhaps most telling to me was when he said, "It wasn't until I thought that I had nothing that I actually realized I had everything. It's like the abyss thing."

*   *   *

And then there is Lauren, whom I have also had the good fortune of meeting in person. For many months, Lauren and I were merely email acquain-tances, as we shot messages back and forth to one another. I struggled mightily with what to say to her at first. How does one address the newly-created prison widow without sounding like a patronizing jackass? I told her to tell me if there was anything I could to do help her, knowing full well that there was nothing I could really do to ease the situation. I knew it was a hollow offer; I'm sure she knew it was, too. I hoped, at least, that she appreciated the human compassion I was willing to offer.

At our first meeting, I wasn't exactly sure what I expected to find. Part of me, I have to admit, expected her to be a snooty and put-upon woman who felt that the world owed her a favor because of the fact that it wasn't her fault her husband had gone to prison, an image I'd parsed together from images of other wives in similar situations that I'd seen in news reports. Or, alternatively, I thought I might discover a depressed and sullen woman who showed defeat at every turn.

Nothing could have been further from the truth. The real Lauren Falcetta was anything but a victim, anything but a sullen widow who blamed the world for all the injustices she was forced to endure. And in the end, it shouldn't have really surprised me in the slightest that she was that way. She's taking her ride on the Wheel of Fortune with an enviable air of grace.

Lauren and the three children met me in a park one summer day. It was, ironically enough, the same park in which I'd had my first meeting with her husband about a year earlier. She was outgoing, laughing, happy. She was a lot like John. Maybe she was putting on a good front, a façade to mask the pain she was really feeling. Or maybe it was something deeper.

Her first request of me was that I not suggest she keep her chin up. She remarked with a laugh that she'd lost count of how many would-be well-wishers had offered her that same advice. "Keep your chin up, Lauren," she said with a wry smile. Never once during the course of our conversation did she sound like the put-upon woman I'd expected to find. Rather, she was living her life as best she could and with as much dignity as she could muster, given the circumstances. How, I asked her, could she be so positive in the face of this whole mess?

"What else am I going to do?" she asked.

And she was right. Given the choice between giving up or moving on, she'd chosen to move on. Not in the sense that she's leaving her husband behind her, but rather in the sense that she's attempting to just move forward and keep things together until the family is reunited. Where does someone find the strength to keep going? Of course, the options are limited. But how easy would it have been for her to fall to the ground and kick and scream and cry, knowing that her life – at least for the next couple of years – was going to consist of monthly visits to see her husband in prison for three hours at a stretch? I still can't answer that question; all I know is that she has it.

She shields her children as best she can from the reality of what their father has done and why he is where he is – and what he's doing there, for that matter – but she and John both know that the day will come when the kids have to learn about one of the legacies that their father has left for them. And when that day arrives, there will be much explaining that needs to be done about what, exactly, Dad was thinking when he made the decision to do what he did. The fact of the matter, though, is that is not the only legacy John will leave his sons. His hope is that they will be able to hold their heads high and be proud of the old man for standing up and doing the right thing, for admitting what he did and for willingly paying the price for it. That is his experience; by choosing to work towards being a better person is what he hopes to do with it. And in so doing, John hopes to make his children proud of him in the way that he himself always sought – always in vain – to make his own father proud of him.

*   *   *

And it is that legacy and the idea that experience is what you do with what you've learned that brings us to the upward turn of the Wheel of Fortune. The word redemption is derived from the Latin *redemptionem*, meaning "a buying back, releasing, ransoming," from the past participle of the verb *redimere*, meaning "to buy back." In an instance such as the one in which John Falcetta currently finds himself, if one manages to achieve full redemption – whatever that looks like – one finds oneself back at the top of the Wheel of Fortune.

But getting to the top of the Wheel is not a matter of buying one's redemption; it's not as easy as going to the local grocery store for a dozen eggs and a carton of orange juice. There is a process to achieving redemption, and that process can take many forms. In some cases, the process can take the shape of a twelve-step recovery program aimed at redeeming those who are prisoners of addiction to lives of spiritual sobriety. In other cases, it can take the shape of travel or work or religious conversion, or any one of an infinite number of other personal betterment vision quests. In John's case, it has taken the dual-pronged shape of a prison sentence coupled with this full and public admission that you have read.

John is the first one to admit that he has made horrible mistakes in his life. But his employers, those who were the ones most victimized by his misdeeds, were some of his most vocal supporters. One former employer said of him, "No matter what really happened at AIG with John, I would still shake his hand and look him in the eye, because I know that he would stand by his word." That doesn't sound like the words of an employer who feels betrayed by the fact that he got duped into hiring somebody who wasn't exactly who he claimed to be, but rather the words of a man who knows John Falcetta's true character.

*   *   *

In the end, however, John is the only one who will decide the course of his future. John will decide the course he must travel to achieve redemption.

Will that path be a long and winding one that ends with his achievement of the elusive state of forgiveness, or will the maze lead nowhere? Or will it lead back to the place in which it began, with another round of schemes?

One is reminded of yet another Shakespearean speech, namely Prospero's closing monologue at the end of *The Tempest*, in which he begs the audience to release him from his personal bondage:

> "Now my charms are all o'erthrown,
> And what strength I have's mine own,
> Which is most faint: now, 'tis true,
> I must be here confined by you,
> Or sent to Naples. Let me not,
> Since I have my dukedom got
> And pardon'd the deceiver, dwell
> In this bare island by your spell;
> But release me from my bands
> With the help of your good hands:
> Gentle breath of yours my sails
> Must fill, or else my project fails,
> Which was to please. Now I want
> Spirits to enforce, art to enchant,
> And my ending is despair,
> Unless I be relieved by prayer,
> Which pierces so that it assaults
> Mercy itself and frees all faults.
> As you from crimes would pardon'd be,
> Let your indulgence set me free."

It's hard to top what is, arguably, one of the most memorable monologues in the English language, and I'm not going to try. Instead, I'm going to suggest that we look at John as a man, flawed from the start, who only seeks to make this world a better place for himself and for his family. In other words, I'd suggest we look at John in much the same way that Shakespeare wanted us to look at Prospero, a man who, at his core, wants what is best for his child.

Just like John.

Prospero is a man who has paid for his sins, who has relinquished much of his raiment, who desires only to be freed from his own guilt by the forgiveness of others. In other words, Shakespeare suggests that Prospero is a man worthy of redemption.

Just like John.

Beyond his devotion to his family and his work, there is a quality that dominates much of John's psychological makeup, namely the fact that he is a conflicted person, a condition he has endured since his earliest days. When he was at AIG, he knew what he was being asked to do with the Bermuda payroll scheme was illegal, but he was unsure as to how best to put a stop to it. It was theft on a massive scale by one of the world's most respected businesses. It was, to a degree, the same thing that he himself was doing. John went to prison; AIG received a $170 billion gift from the federal government.

That inner conflict is what has characterized John's checkered past. He always knew that he was doing something morally wrong, but once he'd slid his way into the position, he excelled at the job, whatever it was. In that success, he was able to hide from the truth that he'd lied to get where he was. But the conflict was always there, always a part of who he was. And who he is today.

That inner conflict filled John with pain and anger until the day that AIG set him free by sending him to prison. He told me, "Going to prison was the best thing to happen to me in my lifetime, because it has literally given me my life back. It's given me a second chance that so many people wish for and never get."

His repeated successes after his repeated dishonesties created a question of scruples, in that they called into question whether the ends justified the means. He wouldn't have been able to get even an initial interview at half the jobs he held over the years if he'd been honest from the start. But he more than proved the fact that he deserved the job once he'd been assigned the work to do. Exaggerated qualifications got him in the door; his abilities kept him there.

Should the misdeeds of a reckless college student be a saddle someone is forced to wear through the rest of their professional life? If John Falcetta had been denied the opportunities he managed to acquire over the course of his professional life, would that have been a more appropriate punishment? Is that true justice? Or does John Falcetta deserve, like Prospero, to be released from his bonds and granted redemption? Only you can decide. And so we return to where we began.

Who is John Falcetta?

I posed that question at the beginning of this work in reference to one of three "useless questions," as Ayn Rand labels them. She deems them "useless" because they are, to a degree, unanswerable, and therefore defy any attempts to answer. However, by the end of *Atlas Shrugged*, we learn who John Galt is and what he stands for. The useless question not only has a valid answer, but also a valuable one.

Who is John Falcetta?

At this moment, he is a head in the window of an office tower at 70 Pine Street, New York City. As such, he's not concerned about all the empty windows surrounding him, nor is he bitter that his head is the only head in a place that he once described to me as a "fucking tower of thieves."

He has become a number. His number is 26772-038, a number that will follow him for the rest of his life, because in the real world, you never pay off your debt to society once you're a convicted felon with an inmate number. Yet as a result of all of this, he is finally free. He is free to reap the fruits of the tree of family, the tree of fatherhood, the tree of friendship. He is free to fight for those who are less fortunate, free to fight for what he believes in and free to fight for what he wants his three boys to believe in.

He believes in America, the country that has made him rich. Rich in belief, as well as rich in hope and freedom. For the first time in his life, John Falcetta is free from ever having to look back over his shoulder to see what horrible incarnation from his past is lurking behind him, waiting to drag him from all that he has found in his life that is good and true. There are no more shadows, no more whispers. There is no more don't-fuck-with-John-Falcetta bravado. Today, he is accepting of the truth in regards to what he made of himself and what that self did to others. In that truth there must be punishment, punishment that he accepts without hesitation or resentment.

A Jesuit priest in Baltimore once told John, "Hell is empty. When you die, you will present yourself to your Maker. At that moment, you will completely and finally realize the shame of your life's sins, and in your shame you will find redemption. This is true for all men. All mankind is redeemed by the power of our Maker."

John related that story to me from prison, and when he had finished telling it, he paused and then grimaced a bit. He raised his eyebrows and said, "So at least I got that going for me."

It was then that I realized that I had my answer to the question that had been nagging me. John Falcetta is every man, from John Galt to George Baily, the man who he says he always wanted to be. Through his shame, he has become what he sought to be in the first place.

Rich.

For sales, editorial information, subsidiary rights information

or a catalog, please write or phone or e-mail

Brick Tower Press

1230 Park Avenue

New York, NY 10128, U.S.

Sales: 1-800-68-BRICK

Tel: 212-427-7139 Fax: 212-860-8852

www.BrickTowerPress.com

email: bricktower@aol.com.

For sales in the United States, please contact

National Book Network

nbnbooks.com

Orders: 800-462-6420

Fax: 800-338-4550

custserv@nbnbooks.com

For sales in the U.K. and Europe please contact our distributor,

Gazelle Book Services

Falcon House, Queens Square

Lancaster, LA1 1RN, UK

Tel: (01524) 68765 Fax: (01524) 63232

email: Sales@gazellebooks.co.uk

For Australian and New Zealand sales please contact

Bookwise International

174 Cormack Road, Wingfield, 5013, South Australia

Tel: 61 (0) 419 340056 Fax: 61 (0)8 8268 1010

email: karen.emmerson@bookwise.com.au